First World War
and Army of Occupation
War Diary
France, Belgium and Germany

36 DIVISION
Divisional Troops
172 Brigade Royal Field Artillery
1 December 1915 - 31 January 1917

WO95/2496/5

The Naval & Military Press Ltd
www.nmarchive.com
Published in association with The National Archives

Published by

The Naval & Military Press Ltd

Unit 10 Ridgewood Industrial Park,

Uckfield, East Sussex,

TN22 5QE England

Tel: +44 (0) 1825 749494

www.naval-military-press.com

www.nmarchive.com

This diary has been reprinted in facsimile from the original. Any imperfections are inevitably reproduced and the quality may fall short of modern type and cartographic standards.

Contents

Document type	Place/Title	Date From	Date To
Heading	WO95/2496/5		
Heading	36th Division 172nd Brigade R.F.A. Dec 1915-Jan 1917. Broken Up		
Heading	36 Div 172nd Bde. R.F.A. Vol: I 121/7910 Dec 15 Jan 17		
War Diary	Bonchon	01/12/1915	31/12/1915
War Diary	Caylux	01/02/1916	21/02/1916
War Diary	Caylux to Pont Remy	22/02/1916	26/02/1916
War Diary	Mailly Maillet	27/02/1916	29/02/1916
Heading	36 172 R.F.A. Vol 3		
Heading	36 172nd Bde: R.F.A. Vol: 2 Jan		
War Diary	Bonchon	01/01/1916	25/01/1916
War Diary	Cayeux	26/01/1916	31/01/1916
War Diary	Mailly Maillet	01/03/1916	31/03/1916
War Diary	In The Field	01/04/1916	25/04/1916
Miscellaneous	Appendix III Copy To Adjutant 172nd Bde R.F.A.		
War Diary	In The Field	26/04/1916	30/04/1916
War Diary	In The Count	01/05/1916	31/05/1916
Miscellaneous	Appendix II To Adjutant 172nd Bde R.F.A.	12/04/1916	12/04/1916
Miscellaneous	Appendix IV Copy Wire Cutting By B/172nd Bde On The 26.4.1916	26/04/1916	26/04/1916
Heading	36th Divisional Artillery. 172nd Brigade. Royal Field Artillery. June 1916		
War Diary	In The Field (Toutencourt)	01/06/1916	14/06/1916
War Diary	Hedauville	15/06/1916	19/06/1916
War Diary	Mesnil	20/06/1916	30/06/1916
Heading	36th Divisional Artillery. 172nd Brigade. Royal Field Artillery. July 1916		
War Diary	Mesnil	01/07/1916	18/07/1916
War Diary	Nordausques	19/07/1916	22/07/1916
War Diary	Neuve Eglise.	23/07/1916	31/07/1916
War Diary	In The Field	01/08/1916	31/08/1916
Operation(al) Order(s)	Operation Orders No. 1. By Lieut. Col. L.E.S. Ward, D.S.O., R.F.A. Commanding Left Group. Appendix I	05/08/1916	05/08/1916
Miscellaneous	Appendix 1. Retaliations.		
Operation(al) Order(s)	Operation Orders No. 2.a By Lieut. Col. L.E.S. Ward, D.S.O. R.F.A. Commanding Left Group. (Appendix IV)	18/08/1916	18/08/1916
Miscellaneous		14/08/1916	14/08/1916
Miscellaneous			
Miscellaneous	Precis Of Arrangements Left Group. (Appendix III)	08/08/1916	08/08/1916
Operation(al) Order(s)	Appendix 2. To L.G. Operation Orders No. 1. (Appendix II)		
War Diary	In The Field	01/09/1916	07/09/1916
Miscellaneous	Appendix 1. To This Office No. 353/172. (App Iv)	06/09/1916	06/09/1916
Miscellaneous	Revised List of Retaliations. (Appendix I)	04/09/1916	04/09/1916
Operation(al) Order(s)	Operation Orders No. 1. By Lieut. Col. L.E.S. Ward, D.S.O., R.F.A. Commanding Left Centre Group. (Appendix 2)	05/09/1916	05/09/1916
Miscellaneous	Table Of Tasks For Operation Order No. 1		

Miscellaneous	353/172. From:- Adjutant 172nd. Brigade. R.F.A. To:- O.C. (Appendix III)	06/09/1916	06/09/1916
War Diary	In The Field	08/09/1916	14/09/1916
Miscellaneous	Appendix To Precis of Arrangements. Left Centre Group. Appendix V	08/09/1916	08/09/1916
Operation(al) Order(s)	Operation Order No. 1. Centre Group. By Lieut. Col. L.E.S. Ward, D.S.O., R.F.A. Appendix VI	09/09/1916	09/09/1916
Miscellaneous			
Operation(al) Order(s)	Operation Order No. 1. Right Group By Lieut. Col. L.E.S. Ward D.S.O. R.F.A. Appendix VII	11/09/1916	11/09/1916
Operation(al) Order(s)	Appendix 1 To Operation Order (Right Group) No. 1. Appendix VIII	13/09/1916	13/09/1916
Miscellaneous	Retaliation In Three Areas, Left, Centre And Right. App IX	14/09/1916	14/09/1916
Operation(al) Order(s)	Appendix 2 To Operation Order No. 1. Right Group. App X	14/09/1916	14/09/1916
War Diary	In The Field	15/09/1916	23/09/1916
Operation(al) Order(s)	Appendix 3 To Operation Order No. 1. Right Group By Lieut. Col. L.E.S. Ward, D.S.O., R.F.A. App XA	17/09/1916	17/09/1916
Operation(al) Order(s)	Operation Order No. 3. By Lieut. Col. L.E.S. Ward D.S.O. R.F.A. Commanding Right Group. (app X B)	21/09/1916	21/09/1916
Miscellaneous	Battery Tasks.		
Operation(al) Order(s)	Amendment To Operation Order No. 1. (App. XC)	22/09/1916	22/09/1916
War Diary	In The Field	24/09/1916	30/09/1916
Operation(al) Order(s)	Operation Order No. 4. By Capt. T.H. Sebag-Montefiore For Officer Commanding Right Group. App XI	27/09/1916	27/09/1916
Miscellaneous	Battery Tasks.		
Operation(al) Order(s)	Operation Order No. 5. By Capt. T.H. Sebag-Montefiore For Officer Commanding Right Group App XII	29/09/1916	29/09/1916
Miscellaneous	Bombardment Table.		
Operation(al) Order(s)	Appendix 1 To Operation Order No. 5. App XIII	29/09/1916	29/09/1916
War Diary	In The Field	01/10/1916	31/10/1916
Operation(al) Order(s)	Operation Order No. 7. By Captain T.H. Sebag-Montefiore. R.F.A. Commanding Right Group Artillery. App I	05/10/1916	05/10/1916
Miscellaneous	Table Of Tasks.		
Operation(al) Order(s)	Appendix 1. To Right Group Operation Order No. 7	05/10/1916	05/10/1916
Operation(al) Order(s)	Operation Order No. 6. By Capt. T.H. Sebag-Montefiore R.F.A. Commanding Right Group. App: II	04/10/1916	04/10/1916
Miscellaneous	Tasks.		
Operation(al) Order(s)	Operation Order No. 8. By Captain T.H. Sebag-Montefiore. R.F.A. Commanding Right Group Artillery. App III	08/10/1916	08/10/1916
Operation(al) Order(s)	Operation Order No. 9. By Major E.W. Bolitho R.F.A. Commanding Right Group App IV	11/10/1916	11/10/1916
Miscellaneous	Tasks.		
Operation(al) Order(s)	Appendix 1 To Right Group Operation Order No. 9	11/10/1916	11/10/1916
War Diary	In The Field	01/11/1916	30/11/1916
Miscellaneous	Appendix To Precis of Arrangements Right Group. App I	05/11/1916	05/11/1916
Miscellaneous	Appendix 5 To Precis Of Arrangements Right Group. App II	05/11/1916	05/11/1916
Miscellaneous	Appendix VII To Precis Of Arrangements Right Group.	17/11/1916	17/11/1916

Miscellaneous	Appendix VIII To Precis Of Arrangements Right Group.	19/11/1916	19/11/1916
Miscellaneous	Appendix IX To Precis of Arrangements Right Group.	20/11/1916	20/11/1916
Operation(al) Order(s)	Operation Orders No. 13. By Lieut. Col. L.E.S. Ward, D.S.O., R.F.A. Commanding Right Group.	22/11/1916	22/11/1916
Miscellaneous	Amendment 1 To Right Group Operation Orders Dated 22.11.1916	22/11/1916	22/11/1916
Miscellaneous	Appendix VI To Precis Of Arrangements Right Group	07/11/1916	07/11/1916
Operation(al) Order(s)	Operation Orders No. 12. By Lieut. Col. L.E.S. Ward, D.S.O., R.F.A. Commanding Right Group. App IV	13/11/1916	13/11/1916
Miscellaneous	Table Of Tasks.		
War Diary	In The Field	01/12/1916	31/12/1916
Miscellaneous	Appendix X To Precis Of Arrangements Right Group.	02/12/1916	02/12/1916
Operation(al) Order(s)	Operation Orders No. 14. By Lieut. Col. L.E.S. Ward, D.S.O., R.F.A. Commanding Centre Group.	11/12/1916	11/12/1916
Operation(al) Order(s)	Operation Orders No. 22 By Lieut. Col. L.E.S. Ward, D.S.O., R.F.A. Commanding 172nd Brigade R.F.A.	31/12/1916	31/12/1916
Operation(al) Order(s)	Operation Orders No. 15. By Lieut. Col. L.E.S. Ward, D.S.O., R.F.A. Commanding Centre Group.	11/12/1916	11/12/1916
Operation(al) Order(s)	Operation Order No. 17., By. Lieut. Col. L.E.S. Ward. D.S.O., R.F.A. Cdg. Centre Group.	25/12/1916	25/12/1916
Operation(al) Order(s)	Operation Orders No. 18. By Lieut. Col. L.E.S. Ward, D.S.O., R.F.A. Commanding Centre Group.	26/12/1916	26/12/1916
Operation(al) Order(s)	Appendix "A" to Centre Group Operation Orders No. 15. Table Of Reliefs Evening 27/28th Dec.	27/12/1916	27/12/1916
Operation(al) Order(s)	Operation Orders No. 19. By Lieut. Col. L.E.S. Ward, D.S.O., R.F.A., Commanding Centre Group.	27/12/1917	27/12/1917
Operation(al) Order(s)	Right Group Orders No. 20 By Lieut. Col. L.E.S. Ward, D.S.O., R.F.A., Commanding Right Group.	28/12/1916	28/12/1916
War Diary	In The Field	01/01/1917	31/01/1917
Operation(al) Order(s)	Appendix 1 To Operation Order No. 22. Right Group.	01/01/1917	01/01/1917
Operation(al) Order(s)	Appendix To Right Group Operation Order No. 20	05/01/1917	05/01/1917

36TH DIVISION

172ND BRIGADE R.F.A.

DEC 1915 - JAN 1917.

BROKEN UP

36 Dn

172nd Bde: R.F.A.

Vol: I

121
7910

Dec '15
Jan '17

Army Form C. 2118

Instructions regarding War Diaries and Intelligence Summaries are contained in F. S. Regs., Part II. and the Staff Manual respectively. Title Pages will be prepared in manuscript.

WAR DIARY
or
~~INTELLIGENCE SUMMARY~~
(Erase heading not required.)

Place	Date	Hour	Summary of Events and Information	Remarks and references to Appendices
Bouchon	1.12.15.		Under instructions from G.O.C. RA., A & B Batteries moved to Long. Reconnaissance for Winter Standings carried out, and Bouchon divided into Sections for purpose of placing 200 horses under cover for Winter. C.O. went to Long in the morning to see A & B. Batteries.	[initials]
	2.12.15.		Further reconnaissance for Winter Standings about Bouchon carried out. C.O. to Long to visit A & B. Batteries and inspect present horse standings. Rain fell during the night and the day was showery. Roads very muddy and horse standings in bad state. Temperature mild. Lt. Champion made a reconnaissance and sketch of the village for scheme for billeting men and horses.	[initials]
	3.12.15.		Slight rain - very muddy - temperature mild Horse Ration 10 lbs. Corn 10 lbs. Hay and in addition 2 lbs. green fodder & 2 lbs of beet. New billeting scheme for men and horses at Bouchon issued to B.Cs together with Map. General Brook visited Bouchon between 2 & 3 p.m. and inspected the sites for Winter Standings. C.O. and Adjutant went to Long to visit A & B. Batteries	[initials]

1875 Wt. W593/826 1,000,000 4/15 J.B.C. & A. A.D.S.S./Forms/C. 2118.

Instructions regarding War Diaries and Intelligence Summaries are contained in F. S. Regs., Part II. and the Staff Manual respectively. Title Pages will be prepared in manuscript.

WAR DIARY
or
~~INTELLIGENCE~~ SUMMARY

(Erase heading not required.)

Army Form C. 2118

Place	Date	Hour	Summary of Events and Information	Remarks and references to Appendices
Bouchon	4.12.15		Showery – temperature mild. Units at Bouchon changing billets and putting horses under cover. C.O. to Long to inspect billets of A + B. Batteries, also to interview the D.D.O. Inspection of harness D. Battery + harness + rifles of two sections of Amm. Column.	LRW
	5.12.15		Examination of claims for damage. – Maire accompanied O.C. in tour of village. Church parade under Canon King. O.C. went to Long. B. Battery moved their horse standings under directions from Col. Paget. Interview with D.D.O. on question of rations. Weather fine and sunny in the morning, but turned to rain in the afternoon – temperature warm.	LRW
	6.12.15		Training recommenced. O.C. to Long to see O.C. B Battery with reference to certain changes in personnel. A.D.V.S. 32nd Division arrived in afternoon and reported that the stable in which C.O's and Adjutant's horses had been billeted had been occupied by a horse with glanders. Stable was disinfected and horses concerned were at once segregated. Weather – fine until 2 pm. when showers set in – temperature mild.	LRW
	7.12.15		C.O. to Cocquerel to meeting of Brigade Commanders at R.A. H.Q. All training stopped pending improvements in billets + erection of horse-standings. Inspection of C Battery billets. Morning – fine, turning to rain in the afternoon. Temperature mild. Lecture by Major Murray – "Night Operations".	LRW
	8.12.15		Work on billets. Inspection of Billets of Amm. Col. Weather wet – temperature slightly colder.	

1875 Wt. W593/826 1,000,000 4/15 J.B.C. & A. A.D.S.S./Forms/C. 2118.

Instructions regarding War Diaries and Intelligence Summaries are contained in F. S. Regs., Part II. and the Staff Manual respectively. Title Pages will be prepared in manuscript.

WAR DIARY
or
~~INTELLIGENCE~~ SUMMARY
(Erase heading not required.)

Army Form C. 2118

Place	Date	Hour	Summary of Events and Information	Remarks and references to Appendices
Bonchon	9.12.15		Work on Billets. R.E. Officer arrived in connection with horse-standings (Winter) G.O.C., R.A. visited ~~Rondon~~ Bonchon to see about Winter Horse Standings. Weather wet - temperature mild	[illegible]
	10.12.15		Work on horse standings commenced. Standings pegged out - drains cut - and chalk accumulation begun. General Nugent accompanied by General Brock arrived to see the horse standings about 11.30 am. Wagons sent for clinkers in the afternoon to "Moulin Blew" L'Etoile. Weather - fair - slight showers - temperature mild. Lecture by Col. "Ward" on relations with the inhabitants of France & "Discipline."	[illegible]
	11.12.15		Work on horse standings continued. C.O. to Divisional Headquarters to Conference of Brigade Commanders. Weather finer - heavy shower in the morning - temperature colder. Lecture to Amm. Col. - use of First Field Dressing - by Medical Officer.	[illegible]
	12.12.15		Work on horse standings continued until 12 noon. French Interpreter Caule joined for duty with the Brigade. Weather fine - no rain. Temperature much colder	[illegible]
	13.12.15		Work on horse standings continued. C.O. to Long to see A & B. Batteries. All Guns 'A' Battery sent to I.O.M. for minor alterations. Weather - fine & cold.	[illegible]

1875 Wt. W593/826 1,000,000 4/15 J.B.C. & A. A.D.S.S./Forms/C. 2118.

Instructions regarding War Diaries and Intelligence Summaries are contained in F. S. Regs., Part II. and the Staff Manual respectively. Title Pages will be prepared in manuscript.

WAR DIARY
or
INTELLIGENCE SUMMARY
(Erase heading not required.)

Army Form C. 2118

Place	Date	Hour	Summary of Events and Information	Remarks and references to Appendices
Bouchon	14.12.15		Work on Horse Standings continued. Lieut. Morgan with 9 vehicles drew bricks. Lieut. Guinness drew poles. C.O. to Long to see B Battery, who were moving into horse standings. Two fields hired for standings (temporary) at Francs 50 & 60 respectively per mensem. 'C' Battery & Amm. Column moved to new horse standings. Weather fine & cold. Lecture to Officers by Captain Gale "Explosives" given in communale school	[initials]
	15.12.15		Work on horse standings continued. Posts put in and brick drains commenced. 7 wagons sent to draw bricks – bricks of bad kind and useless for designed purpose – report made to R.A. H.Q. Pioneer Battalion. 3 Ammunition Wagons handed over to 154th Bde. Weather – no rain during the morning, but drizzle after midday – temperature cold. 'C' Battery F.S. Marching Order Parade – all day.	[initials]
	16.12.15		Work on horse lines continued – one motor lorry allotted to Brigade employed drawing bricks. General Brock inspected Billets at Long and Bouchon. Weather – dull & cold – no rain. Lecture by Captain Murray (Major Murray's brother) to all officers "Section of the line".	[initials]

1875 Wt. W593/826 1,000,000 4/15 J.B.C. & A. A.D.S.S./Forms/C. 2118.

Army Form C. 2118

Instructions regarding War Diaries and Intelligence Summaries are contained in F. S. Regs., Part II. and the Staff Manual respectively. Title Pages will be prepared in manuscript.

WAR DIARY
or
~~INTELLIGENCE~~ SUMMARY
(Erase heading not required.)

Place	Date	Hour	Summary of Events and Information	Remarks and references to Appendices
Barchon	17.12.15		Fatigues on horse-standings continued. Laying bricks on first standing commenced. Motor Lorry employed fetching bricks. Wood for horse-troughs received. Weather - steady fine rain, most of the day. Temperature - milder than yesterday	[initials]
	18.12.15		Fatigues on horse standings - instructions received to lengthen standings for each horse from 9 feet to 11 feet. C.O. to [illegible] to inspect sanitary arrangement of B Battery. Adjutant to Abbeville to make arrangements for supplies for 'Dry Canteen.' 'C' Battery's guns sent to I.O.M. A & B. batteries guns completed. Weather - foggy in the morning till about 9.30 am - no rain - temperature normal.	[initials]
	19.12.15		General holiday. First game of league competition. 'C' beat 'D' by 4 goals to 1.	[initials]
	20.12.15		Fatigues on horse standings continued. Staff ride - Bde. Commander. Adjutant. B.C's & orderly officer met General Brock at Fontaine. Scheme carried out on Liercourt - Hedlencourt line.	[initials]
	21.12.15		Fatigues on horse standings. General Brock inspected work up to date. Instructions for alteration in mobilization scheme received. Weather - very wet & cold - steady rain all day.	[initials]

1875 Wt. W593/826 1,000,000 4/15 J.B.C. & A. A.D.S.S./Forms/C. 2118.

Instructions regarding War Diaries and Intelligence Summaries are contained in F. S. Regs., Part II. and the Staff Manual respectively. Title Pages will be prepared in manuscript.

WAR DIARY
or
~~INTELLIGENCE SUMMARY~~
(Erase heading not required.)

Army Form C. 2118

Place	Date	Hour	Summary of Events and Information	Remarks and references to Appendices
Bouchon	22.12.15		Fatigues on horse standings. Inspection of Sanitary areas A & D Batteries & Amm. Column. C.O. to Long in the morning re certain claims for damages to billets there. Weather wet during the morning but rain ceased during the afternoon. Temperature - mild. Lecture by Major Murray, who gave the first of a series on Gunnery	[illegible]
	23.12.15		Fatigues on horse standings. Malleining of Brigade completed. Weather - a few slight showers - rather fine - temperature mild	[illegible]
	24.12.15		Fatigues on Horse Standings - General Lecky C.R.A. 13th Corps inspected horse standings. Work on billets also proceeding. Weather - showery - temperature mild. All guns completed by I.O.M. Lecture to officers "Organization of the British Army" Lt. Col. Ward.	[illegible]
	25.12.15		Christmas Day - General Holiday. Brigade League football match. A.2. v Amm. Col. result 3-1 in favour of Amm. Col. Divine service 12 noon. Heavy showers - temperature mild	[illegible]
	26.12.15		Fatigues on horse standings. General Allenby (Corps Commander). Divisional Commander & C.R.A. inspected Winter Horse Standings at 10.30 a.m. Weather fine - temperature mild - one slight shower.	[illegible]
	27.12.15		Fatigues on horse standings till mid-day. General half holiday. League games D v Amm. Col. result Amm. Col. 4 goals D Nil. A v B result A. 1 goal B Nil	[illegible]

1875 Wt. W593/826 1,000,000 4/15 J.B.C. & A. A.D.S.S./Forms/C. 2118.

Instructions regarding War Diaries and Intelligence Summaries are contained in F. S. Regs., Part II. and the Staff Manual respectively. Title Pages will be prepared in manuscript.

WAR DIARY
or
INTELLIGENCE SUMMARY

(Erase heading not required.)

Army Form C. 2118

Place	Date	Hour	Summary of Events and Information	Remarks and references to Appendices
Lanchen	28.12.15		Work on horse standings continued. Lecture - second of series on "Shell & Explosives" by Captain Gale. Weather - fine - no rain - temperature mild	[illegible]
	29.12.15		Fatigues on horse standings. Weather - no rain - temperature mild	[illegible]
	30.12.15		Fatigues on horse standings & Billets. Weather - fine - no rain - temperature mild	[illegible]
	31.12.15		Horse standings completed - 140 horses of Amm Col. put on new standings. Lecture No. 3. Gunnery by Major Murray. Weather showery - slightly colder.	[illegible]

1875 Wt. W593/826 1,000,000 4/15 J.B.C. & A. A.D.S.S./Forms/C. 2118.

Instructions regarding War Diaries and Intelligence Summaries are contained in F. S. Regs., Part II. and the Staff Manual respectively. Title Pages will be prepared in manuscript.

WAR DIARY
or
~~INTELLIGENCE SUMMARY~~
(Erase heading not required.)

172 Brigade R.F.A.

Army Form C. 2118

Place	Date	Hour	Summary of Events and Information	Remarks and references to Appendices
Cayeux	1.2.16		Section Training in the Field. Weather fine & cold	RD
	2.2.16		Section Training. O.C. R.A. visited horse lines of B C & D Batteries. Lecture "Ammunition" by Major Bolitho. Weather fine & cold	RD
	3.2.16		Section Training. Weather fine - not so cold as previous days. Strong S.W. wind blowing	RD
	4.2.16		Section Training. Divisional Entertainers Concert for the Bde. Weather overcast, strong wind - cold	RD
	5.2.16		Section Training. Weather - very fine & warm	RD
	6.2.16		Divine Service. Medical Inspection. Weather windy & cold.	RD
	7.2.16		Battery Training. Lecture "S.O.S." by Captain Montespire. Weather windy - heavy shower in morning - cold	RD
	8.2.16		Battery Training. Weather - windy - showery & cold	RD
	9.2.16		Battery Training. Lecture "Map reading and sketching" by Lieut. Champion. Weather fine & warmer	RD
	10.2.16		Battery Training. Weather fine & cold.	RD
	11.2.16		Rain interfered with the general scheme of parades. Lecture "Gallipoli" by Lieut Col P. Wheatley, 173rd Bde R.F.A. Weather very wet	RD
	12.2.16		Battery Training. Weather fine temperature mild	RD
	13.2.16		Divine Service. Weather wet in the morning. fine afternoon - temperature cold.	RD

Instructions regarding War Diaries and Intelligence Summaries are contained in F. S. Regs., Part II. and the Staff Manual respectively. Title Pages will be prepared in manuscript.

WAR DIARY
or
~~INTELLIGENCE SUMMARY~~
(Erase heading not required.)

Army Form C. 2118

1/3 Brigade R.F.A.

Place	Date	Hour	Summary of Events and Information	Remarks and references to Appendices
Cayeux	14.7.16		A & B batteries fired the first line practice shoot. Weather very windy and temperature cold. Lecture "Interior Economy" by Major Murray. 2/Lts. R.H. Hose and D.P. Dickson joined the Bde & were posted to B & C Batteries respectively.	RO
	15.7.16		C & D Batts fired the first line practice shoot. Weather fine but very windy in the morning, rain during the afternoon – very cold all day.	RO
	16.7.16		During the morning training according to Battery programme. 1st line shoot for A & B batteries postponed owing to weather conditions. Lecture "Ammunition" Major Boileau. Weather – very windy – heavy rain during the morning – temperature cold.	RO
	17.7.16		Training according to Battery schemes during the morning. Firing of line 1 for A & B & C batteries again postponed. Weather – windy but fine – temperature warmer.	RO
	18.7.16		The state of the weather prevented all chance of carrying out training programme. Lectures, laying tests & instructions to NCOs was substituted for outdoor work. Weather – continual rain and wind – temperature cold.	RO
	19.7.16		Training continued under better weather conditions – temperature much warmer.	RO
	20.7.16		Divine service & parade for G.O.C.R.A.	RO
	21.7.16		All batteries fired first line under Battery Commanders & a second series was taken by junior subalterns. Weather dull & very cold.	RO

1875 Wt. W593/826 1,000,000 4/15 J.B.C. & A. A.D.S.S./Forms/C. 2118.

Instructions regarding War Diaries and Intelligence Summaries are contained in F. S. Regs., Part II. and the Staff Manual respectively. Title Pages will be prepared in manuscript.

WAR DIARY
or
~~INTELLIGENCE SUMMARY~~
(Erase heading not required.)

Army Form C. 2118

142 Brigade R.F.A.

Place	Date	Hour	Summary of Events and Information	Remarks and references to Appendices
Cayeux to Pont Remy	22.2.16		Bde. less Ammunition Column marched from Cayeux via Rue & Abbeville to Pont Remy where billets were occupied. Distance about 23 miles. Weather fine but very cold - heavy fall of snow during the afternoon.	
	23.2.16		Brigade marched from Pont Remy to Bernois about 14 miles. Difficult march owing to frozen and slippery state of road. Weather freezing - much snow.	
	24.2.16		Bde marched from Bernois to Puchevillers - distance 12 miles. Another difficult march owing to state of roads. Weather - partial thaw & heavy frost in the evening	
	25.2.16		Bde. marched from Puchevillers to Acheux Wood where bivouac was occupied. Most trying march - heavy snow & blizzard - very cold	
	26.2.16		Bde distributed as follows. Brigade & Battery Commanders with details at Mailly Maillet. Parties under instructions with 4th Divisional Artillery. Remainder of Bde including Bde. Ammunition Column at Acheux Wood. Weather - freezing - some snow.	
Mailly Maillet	27.2.16		Distributions as above. A and B batteries at work on their gun positions. OC visited Acheux Wood where general conditions were deplorable. Weather - slight thaw but still very cold. 'A' battery moved into position near Engelbelmer.	
	28.2.16.		A battery registered 62 rounds fired. One section each of C & D Batteries went into action. 'B' Battery arrived on their position but did not go into action as the gun emplacements were not ready. Weather - thaw set in making country very wet. Temperature - less severe	
	29.2.16		B. C & D batteries registered. GOCRA visited all battery positions & several OPs. Remaining sections of C & D Batteries came into action during the night. 134th Battery put into left front, tactically as a temporary measure until completion of registration by B. Weather - thawed considerably - some rain - temperature warmer.	

1875 Wt. W593/826 1,000,000 4/15 J.B.C. & A. A.D.S.S./Forms/C. 2118.

36 4

172nd Bde: R.F.A.
Vol: 2

Tan

Instructions regarding War Diaries and Intelligence Summaries are contained in F. S. Regs., Part II. and the Staff Manual respectively. Title Pages will be prepared in manuscript.

WAR DIARY

or

~~INTELLIGENCE SUMMARY~~

(Erase heading not required.)

172nd Brigade R.F.A.

Army Form C. 2118

Place	Date	Hour	Summary of Events and Information	Remarks and references to Appendices
Bouchon	1.1.16		Brigade allotted use of Divisional Baths. D Battery went from 10–12 a.m. A Battery 12 noon to 1 pm. & 2 pm–3 pm. Amm. Col. 3–5 pm. General fatigues on billets. Weather showery – temperature cold. Adjutant to Divisional H.Q. for Lecture	[illegible]
	2.1.16		Divine Service in Ecole Communale at 12.30 pm. Football league games Amm. Col. 3 goals B NIL. A Battery 3 goals H.Q. NIL. Weather showery – more wind – temperature normal.	[illegible]
	3.1.16		Lt Col. L. E. S. Ward went to L'Etoile in temporary command of D.A. Ulster Division. Major A.D. Murray took over temporary command of Brigade. Weather fine – temperature mild. Bde. started training again.	[illegible]
	4.1.16		Lt Col. L. E. S. Ward returned from L'Etoile. Training under Battery arrangements. Weather fine – temperature mild	[illegible]
	5.1.16		Battery training. Third lecture by Capt. Gale "Shells". Weather fine – temperature mild.	[illegible]
	6.1.16		Brigade Route March. Bde assembled at Villers-sous-Ailly and marched to Domart en Ponthieu via Vauchelles. Water & feed at Domart and returned to Bouchon by way of Monflers – distance about 15 miles. Weather – slight drizzle – temperature mild.	[illegible]

1875 Wt. W593/826 1,000,000 4/15 J.B.C. & A. A.D.S.S./Forms/C. 2118.

Instructions regarding War Diaries and Intelligence Summaries are contained in F. S. Regs., Part II. and the Staff Manual respectively. Title Pages will be prepared in manuscript.

WAR DIARY 172nd Bde R.F.A.

or

~~INTELLIGENCE SUMMARY~~

(Erase heading not required.)

Army Form C. 2118

Place	Date	Hour	Summary of Events and Information	Remarks and references to Appendices
Bonchon	7.1.16		Battery Training. Weather – wet – heavy rain in the afternoon – temperature colder. Lecture "Divisional Staff organization" Lt. R.M. Durant	BGW
	8.1.16		Battery Training. Weather – fine – temperature cold.	BGW
	9.1.16		General Holiday. Football League D 2 goals H.Q. 1. Amm Col. 10 goals A 1. Very fine day.	BGW
	10.1.16		Battery Training. Major Murray left on course of Co-operation of Artillery & Infantry. Weather – rainy during the morning, no rain in the afternoon – temperature cold.	BGW
	11.1.16		Battery Training. G.O.C. R.A. watched C Battery at field exercises. G.O.C. made horse inspection of Amm. Col. + C + D Batteries. Weather – showery – temperature mild	BGW
	12.1.16		Battery Training. C.O. carried out reconnaissance for Brigade Training Scheme for Thursday. General & Special Ideas issued with assembly orders. G.O.C. R.A. carried out horse inspection of A + B Batteries at Long. Weather – frosty in early morning – slight rain during the afternoon – temperature mild. 4th lecture by Capt. Gale (Ammunition)	BGW
	13.1.16		Brigade Scheme of Training No. 1 carried out (see Training File) General Brook was present. 35 Remounts arrived from Railhead. Weather – stormy – heavy hail showers during the afternoon – temperature cold.	BGW

1875 Wt. W593/826 1,000,000 4/15 J.B.C. & A. A.D.S.S./Forms/C. 2118.

Instructions regarding War Diaries and Intelligence Summaries are contained in F. S. Regs., Part II. and the Staff Manual respectively. Title Pages will be prepared in manuscript.

WAR DIARY
or
~~INTELLIGENCE SUMMARY~~
(Erase heading not required.)

172nd Bde RFA

Army Form C. 2118

Place	Date	Hour	Summary of Events and Information	Remarks and references to Appendices
Barchon	14.1.16		Battery Training. C.O. & inspected C & D Batteries at smoke helmet drill. Instructions received for C.O. & Adjutant to hold themselves in readiness to proceed to the "line" for instruction. Lecture "March Discipline" by the Adjutant. Weather - cold & fine	SSW
	15.1.16		C.O. & Adjt left at 8.30 am on visit to the front. Major Bolitho left in charge of Brigade. Weather - mild & overcast - little fine rain	SSW
	16.1.16		Church Parade 12.30 am. Football match in afternoon at Long 'B' beat C. by 2 - 1 goals. Weather overcast - some fine rain in morning, but mild. Major Murray returned & took over charge of Brigade	SSW
	17.1.16		Battery Training. Weather - fine - temperature mild.	SSW
	18.1.16		Battery Training. C.O. & Adjutant returned from visit to front. Weather - wet & cold.	SSW
	19.1.16		Battery Training. Orderly Officer proceeded to Cayeux to see about new Billets. Lecture by Major Murray on "Calibration". Weather - fine	SSW
	20.1.16		Brigade Training Scheme II carried out "An advance & occupation of a subsequent position. Weather - fine in the morning - a heavy shower about 1. pm	SSW

1875 Wt. W593/826 1,000,000 4/15 J.B.C. & A. A.D.S.S./Forms/C. 2118.

Instructions regarding War Diaries and Intelligence Summaries are contained in F. S. Regs., Part II. and the Staff Manual respectively. Title Pages will be prepared in manuscript.

WAR DIARY
or
~~INTELLIGENCE SUMMARY~~

(Erase heading not required.)

172nd Bde RFA

Army Form C. 2118

Place	Date	Hour	Summary of Events and Information	Remarks and references to Appendices
Bouchon	21.1.16		Battery Training. Preliminary orders for move of Brigade to new training area issued. Concluding lecture on "Ammunition" by Capt. Gale. Weather – dull & cold – no rain.	[initials]
	22.1.16		Battery Training. Preparations for move. Weather – cloudy in morning – slight shower during the afternoon – temperature mild.	[initials]
	23.1.16		Brigade, less Amm. Col. left Bouchon & Long for new training area marching via Pont Remy – Bray – Cambron & halted for the night at Boismont & Mons. Billeting order Bde H.Q. } A Battery } B Battery } Boismont; C Battery } D Battery } Mons.	[initials]
			Brigade Ammunition Column left Bouchon & proceeded to new billeting area at St. Leger. Weather – fine & warm.	
	24.1.16		Brigade left march billets at 7 am – concentrated at Lanchères & proceeding via Wathiehurt & Hurt reached Cayeux at 10 am. Remainder of day spent in settling into new billets. Weather – slight drizzle in the early morning – remainder of day fine – temperature mild	
	25.1.16		Settling into Billets at Cayeux. C.O. went round all Billets. Weather – fine – temperature cold.	

1875 Wt. W593/826 1,000,000 4/15 J.B.C. & A. A.D.S.S./Forms/C. 2118.

Instructions regarding War Diaries and Intelligence Summaries are contained in F. S. Regs., Part II. and the Staff Manual respectively. Title Pages will be prepared in manuscript.

WAR DIARY

172nd Bde RFA

or

~~INTELLIGENCE SUMMARY~~

(Erase heading not required.)

Army Form C. 2118

Place	Date	Hour	Summary of Events and Information	Remarks and references to Appendices
Cayeux	26.1.16		Settling into Billets. Weather fine & cold. Lecture "Visit to the front" by Lt Col. L.E.S. Ward	LESW
	27.1.16		Training recommenced. Distribution of Brigade on this date Bde H.Q. } Cayeux A.B.C.&D. Batts } Bde Amm Col. St Leger Weather cloudy & cold.	LESW
	28.1.16		Training Continued. General Jackson, Artillery adviser to 14th Corps visited the Brigade. Lecture "Horse Mastership" by Capt. Montifiore. Weather – cloudy & mild	LESW
	29.1.16		Training continued. Weather – very fine & warm	LESW
	30.1.16		Divine Service under command of Major E.W. Bolitho. 2/Lt. R.M. Durant left for course of gunnery at Havernas. Weather foggy & cold.	
	31.1.16		Training continued. M.O. reports a lot of scabies in the Brigade. Special measures taken. Lecture "Vehicles" by Capt Gale	LESW

L.E.S. Ward

Lt Col RFA
OC 172nd Bde RFA
3/2/1916

1875 Wt. W593/826 1,000,000 4/15 J.B.C. & A. A.D.S.S./Forms/C. 2118.

Instructions regarding War Diaries and Intelligence Summaries are contained in F. S. Regs., Part II. and the Staff Manual respectively. Title Pages will be prepared in manuscript.

799/264

WAR DIARY
or
INTELLIGENCE SUMMARY
(Erase heading not required.)

177th Bde RFA

Army Form C. 2118

976

Place	Date	Hour	Summary of Events and Information	Remarks and references to Appendices
[illegible]	1.3.16		14th Bde entirely withdrawn during the night 29th-1st. All communication - position stores etc taken over. All batteries registered during the day. Weather cloudy temperature warmer.	[illegible]
	2.3.16		OC visited A Battery OP and Battalion Headquarters in the trenches. B battery continued to register. [illegible] rounds of [illegible] were fired on D battery position. C Battery were also fired on by a [illegible] battery - [illegible] line [illegible] shot. During the night C Battery lines fired on [illegible] [illegible] zone taken up for SOS barrage. Weather - cloudy - some rain temperature cold	[illegible]
	3.3.16		OC visited OP of C & D Batteries and saw day barrage fired. Inspection of Billets & sanitation. In afternoon inspection of forward wagon lines behind [illegible] Wood. Weather - cloudy - slight rain - temperature cold.	[illegible]
	4.3.16		Owing to state of weather heavy fall of snow. Artillery on both sides was inactive - due to impossibility of observation & fire. A Battery withdrawn from left group and placed under orders of Right group tactically. Weather - much snow - very cold.	[illegible]
	5.3.16		OC visited headquarters of two battalions in trenches. German Artillery showed some activity. D/177 (Howitzers) came into the group tactically. Rear wagon lines shelled at [illegible]. Three horses severely wounded. Weather clear, bright and some snow. Temperature cold.	[illegible]

1875 Wt. W593/826 1,000,000 4/15 J.B.C. & A. A.D.S.S./Forms/C. 2118.

Instructions regarding War Diaries and Intelligence Summaries are contained in F. S. Regs., Part II. and the Staff Manual respectively. Title Pages will be prepared in manuscript.

WAR DIARY
or
~~INTELLIGENCE SUMMARY~~
(Erase heading not required.)

Army Form C. 2118

977

Place	Date	Hour	Summary of Events and Information	Remarks and references to Appendices
Mailly-Maillet	6.3.16		Very little activity on either side during the morning owing to difficulties of observation. Clear afternoon all batteries fired. Brigade Amm. Col. moved from Acheux to Bertrancourt. Weather snow in morning, fine afternoon. Temperature - not so cold.	BLW
	7.3.16		During the night 6th/7th the enemy shelled our trenches 60-63 (see appendix I). D.C.R.A. visited O.P. during the afternoon. Very quiet day - little activity on both sides. Weather - freezing during night - steady thaw - temperature warmer.	BLW
	8.3.16		Quiet day. O.C. to Bertrancourt to see new Billets of Bde Amm. Column. Operation undertaken on hostile transport reported to be using the Beaumont Hamel - Station Road. Firing commenced at 7.11 pm and continued for 20 minutes. Following batteries were employed from left front. C/172. Beaumont Hamel - Station Road D/154 (How) Right section Beaumont Hamel - Station Road. Left section - crossroad in Beaumont Hamel. 40 rounds per Battery were expended. Weather fine - thaw during the day. Temperature - cold. During night - hard frost.	BLW
	9.3.16		O.C. to R.A.H.Q. for conference of all Brigade Commanders. Day generally quiet - comparatively little activity of Artillery on both sides. Weather - hard frost in the evening with a fall of snow during the night. Temperature - very cold.	BLW

Instructions regarding War Diaries and Intelligence Summaries are contained in F. S. Regs., Part II. and the Staff Manual respectively. Title Pages will be prepared in manuscript.

WAR DIARY
or
~~INTELLIGENCE~~ SUMMARY
(Erase heading not required.)

Army Form C. 2118

978

Place	Date	Hour	Summary of Events and Information	Remarks and references to Appendices
Mailly Maillet	10.3.16		CO visited Battalion Head quarters of both sectors and various observation posts. Normal activity of Artillery during the day. B/152 carried out wire cutting practice (Appendix II) 150 rounds were used. During the night heavy artillery fire was heard in the direction of Thiepval. Weather misty & cold	LRLW
	11.3.16		Normal activity. CO instructions issued to all batteries & copies to flanking Bdes. Quiet night. Weather - misty & cold	LRLW
	12.3.16		Hostile Artillery was a little more active than usual especially on the [illegible]. In evening intimation received that one section of A/153 would come into the group tactically. One gun 1st Siege battery 6" Howitzer was also added to the group. Weather fine - temperature warmer & a large thaw	LRLW
	13.3.16		Normal artillery activity. Artillery Advisor to 8th Corps visited the positions of C & D batteries. CO to Acheux for Artillery Conference. Weather warm & fine	LRLW
	14.3.16		Hostile artillery rather more active than usual. A rapid burst of fire was employed against the Tenderloin. C/152 retaliated on the enemy trenches at 67. B/152 carried out wire cutting (see Appendix III) 100 rounds were used. Weather - fine & warm	LRLW
	15.3.16		Enemy shewed activity and bombarded Auchonvillers twice during morning. At 2 pm the divisional Artillery asked to arrange a retaliation of Beaumont Hamel	LRLW
				LRLW

Instructions regarding War Diaries and Intelligence Summaries are contained in F. S. Regs., Part II. and the Staff Manual respectively. Title Pages will be prepared in manuscript.

WAR DIARY
or
~~INTELLIGENCE SUMMARY~~
(Erase heading not required.)

Army Form C. 2118

979

Place	Date	Hour	Summary of Events and Information	Remarks and references to Appendices
Mailly Maillet	15.3.16 (cont'd)		Result of registration of A/153 received and instructions for 20-[illegible] issued to this part of group. Composition of group on this date. B/172 C/172 D/172 D/154 A/153 one section 16th Siege Batty. 1 gun	[illegible]
	16.3.16		Enemy again shelled [illegible] and Infantry called for retaliation. Two officers from Bde. Ammunition Column brought up for instruction with C/[illegible] Batt. Weather cloudy - temperature mild.	[illegible]
	17.3.16		Normal activity during the morning. About 4pm enemy shelled our trenches in front of the Redan. Infantry called for retaliation which was carried out by D/172 + D/154 (Howitzer). About 5.30pm the major reported the enemy were shelling our right sector and asked for Howitzer retaliation which was carried out on the Hawthorn Redoubt. C/172 carried out wire cutting on Q[illegible] 150 rounds were used (appendix IV). Weather - fine temperature mild	[illegible]

Instructions regarding War Diaries and Intelligence Summaries are contained in F. S. Regs., Part II. and the Staff Manual respectively. Title Pages will be prepared in manuscript.

WAR DIARY
or
INTELLIGENCE SUMMARY
(Erase heading not required.)

Army Form C. 2118

a 60

Place	Date	Hour	Summary of Events and Information	Remarks and references to Appendices
Mailly Maillet	18.3.16		Normal activity of both artilleries. At 1.0 pm enemy shelled our trenches opposite the Redan. Infantry called for retaliation which was given by B Battery. Shortly afterwards the enemy shelled [illegible] right sector and retaliation was called for which was given by C Battery who fired on the left barrage. On appearance of crossed [illegible] lights (from enemy trenches) C Battery increased their rate of fire. Weather fine & warm	[illegible]
	19.3.16		A quiet day – very little artillery activity. One section X Battery RHA joined for purpose of giving instruction in wire cutting. Major A.D. [illegible] left the Bde. 17 Bgde to [illegible] temporarily the duties of Bde Major. Weather – cloudy – temperature mild. Leave opened for 7 officers.	[illegible]
	20.3.16		Normal activity – B Battery carried out instruction wire cutting practice (Appendix V). 11 Officers of 1st, 2nd & 3rd Division arrived for instructional attachment	[illegible]
	21.3.16		Normal activity. A Battery carried out wire cutting practice (Appendix VI). GOCRA visited all battery positions in the front. Weather overcast & cold	[illegible]
	22.3.16		Quiet day. C Battery carried out wire cutting instruction (Appendix VII). Weather – slight rain – temperature cold.	[illegible]

1875 Wt. W593/826 1,000,000 4/15 J.B.C. & A. A.D.S.S./Forms/C. 2118.

Instructions regarding War Diaries and Intelligence Summaries are contained in F. S. Regs., Part II and the Staff Manual respectively. Title Pages will be prepared in manuscript.

WAR DIARY
or
INTELLIGENCE SUMMARY
(Erase heading not required.)

Army Form C. 2118

981

Place	Date	Hour	Summary of Events and Information	Remarks and references to Appendices
[illegible]	[illegible]		Normal activity. Wire cutting [illegible] cancelled by order from R.A.H.Q. [illegible] activity by night. Weather overcast & cloudy - temperature cold. [illegible] fall of snow during night 13-14.	[illegible]
	[illegible]		[illegible] very quiet throughout day & night - due to weather conditions which precluded all observation. Weather dull & overcast - [illegible] fall - temperature cold. [illegible] stopped.	[illegible]
	[illegible]		Quiet day and night - practically no firing by either Artillery. Weather [illegible] with strong thaw - temperature - warmer but still cold.	[illegible]
	[illegible]		Very quiet day & night. Lt. Barrett & Marshall joined for duty & were posted to B/172. Weather - rain during the morning but cleared at mid-day. Temperature cold - some wind.	[illegible]
	[illegible]		Normal activity. Weather cloudy, rain after 3 pm. Windy, temperature cold.	[illegible]
	[illegible]		Normal activity. Weather cold & overcast - slight frost during the night.	[illegible]
	[illegible]		[illegible] the Artillery work on either side. B/172 battery reported that a [illegible] captive balloon had broken loose about 3 pm. Weather - fine bright morning - snow in the afternoon.	[illegible]
	[illegible]		Normal activity - weather fine - temperature warmer. Information received that the 36th Divisional Artillery would be relieved by the 31st Divisional Artillery.	[illegible]

1875 Wt. W593/826 1,000,000 4/15 J.B.C. & A. A.D.S.S./Forms/C. 2118.

Instructions regarding War Diaries and Intelligence Summaries are contained in F. S. Regs., Part II. and the Staff Manual respectively. Title Pages will be prepared in manuscript.

WAR DIARY
or
INTELLIGENCE SUMMARY
(Erase heading not required.)

Army Form C. 2118

982

Place	Date	Hour	Summary of Events and Information	Remarks and references to Appendices
[illegible]	[illegible]		Normal activity – one section per battery 170th Bde. 3rd Divisional Artillery arrived to take over from corresponding units 172nd Bde. Weather fine – temperature warm.	[illegible]

1875 Wt. W593/826 1,000,000 4/15 J.B.C. & A. A.D.S.S./Forms/C. 2118.

Instructions regarding War Diaries and Intelligence Summaries are contained in F. S. Regs., Part II. and the Staff Manual respectively. Title Pages will be prepared in manuscript.

XXXVI

WAR DIARY
or
~~INTELLIGENCE SUMMARY~~
(Erase heading not required.)

172nd Bde RFA

April 1916

Army Form C. 2118

Vol. 4

Place	Date	Hour	Summary of Events and Information	Remarks and references to Appendices
In the Field	1.4.16		31st Divisional Artillery relieved Brigade by Sections 170th Bde take up area	[illegible]
	2.4.16		Relief by 170th Bde RFA completed by 10 am. 172nd Bde moved into Toutencourt in Reserve. Weather very fine & warm.	[illegible]
	3.4.16		Distribution of Brigade. Four batteries and Amm. Column at Toutencourt. Fatigue parties from batteries bivouaced at Mesnil. Weather very fine & warm. Major A.D. Murray rejoined Brigade for duty.	[illegible]
	4.4.16		Corps Commander 10th Corps visited camp & walked round horse lines. Weather cloudy - temperature cold.	[illegible]
	5.4.16		Work on 4th Army Staff Ride continued. R.E. put in horse troughs & pump at Toutencourt. Weather cloudy - temperature very cold	[illegible]
	6.4.16		CO Brigade accompanied C.R.A. Division on inspection of O.Ps in connection with 4th Army Staff Ride. Weather fine - temperature cold	[illegible]
	7.4.16		Nothing to note. Weather fine - temperature cold.	
	8.4.16		Lecture to all B.Cs & one subaltern per battery on co-operation of Artillery and aeroplane given by an officer of R.F.C. Weather fine - temperature cold. 'A' Battery cut wire (Appendix I).	[illegible] [illegible]

1875 Wt. W593/826 1,000,000 4/15 J.B.C. & A. A.D.S.S./Forms/C. 2118.

Instructions regarding War Diaries and Intelligence Summaries are contained in F. S. Regs., Part II. and the Staff Manual respectively. Title Pages will be prepared in manuscript.

WAR DIARY
or
~~INTELLIGENCE SUMMARY~~
(Erase heading not required.)

Army Form C. 2118

Place	Date	Hour	Summary of Events and Information	Remarks and references to Appendices
In the Field	9.4.16		Inspection of work on positions in connection with 4th Army Staff Ride. Major A.D. Murray left the Brigade to take over command of 173rd Bde RFA. Weather fine - temperature warmer.	[illegible]
	10.4.16		Work on 4th Army Staff Ride continued. Orderly Officer proceeded to Mesnil in connection with Bde communications. Weather fine & warm	[illegible]
	11.4.16		Work as above. Weather fine & warm. 'B' Battery carried out wire cutting practice (appendix II)	[illegible]
	12.4.16		Artillery Adviser 10th Corps (General Budworth) inspected work done in connection with 4th Army Staff Ride. Weather - heavy rain - temperature cold	[illegible]
	13.4.16		Reconnaissance for single gun positions for general defence scheme. Weather fine but very windy - temperature still cold. All leave stopped.	[illegible]
	14.4.16		Further reconnaissance of single gun positions sites for which were finally decided on. Weather very wet & cold.	[illegible]
	15.4.16		Normal. Weather cold, windy & much rain.	[illegible]
	16.4.16		Normal. Weather fine & warm	[illegible]
	17.4.16		C.O. inspected all horses. Weather - windy - much rain and temperature very cold	[illegible]

Army Form C. 2118

Instructions regarding War Diaries and Intelligence Summaries are contained in F. S. Regs., Part II. and the Staff Manual respectively. Title Pages will be prepared in manuscript.

WAR DIARY
or
~~INTELLIGENCE~~ SUMMARY
(Erase heading not required.)

Place	Date	Hour	Summary of Events and Information	Remarks and references to Appendices
In the Field	18.4.16		Normal. Heavy rain - very cold.	[illegible]
	19.4.16		A Battery carried out wire cutting practice (appendix III) Heavy rain - very cold.	[illegible]
	20.4.16		First casualty suffered by Brigade - one man of 'C' Battery being wounded by machine gun fire. Weather fine - temperature warmer.	[illegible]
	21.4.16		Good Friday - trench bridge received and passed to D Battery for experimental purposes. Weather - fine in the morning, but rain again in the afternoon - temperature cold.	[illegible]
	22.4.16		One subsection of D Battery turned out for experiment with trench bridge - conclusions - bridge too heavy and not portable enough for Field Artillery purposes. Weather - heavy rain - temperature cold.	[illegible]
	23.4.16		Accompanied C.R.A. & Brigade Major on reconnaissance of forward gun positions. Weather - great improvement - fine & much warmer.	[illegible]
	24.4.16		General Holiday. Weather very good - fine & warm	[illegible]
	25.4.16		Further reconnaissance of gun positions (forward) A battery experimented with another form of trench bridge. G.O.C.R.A. inspected wagon lines. Weather fine & warm.	[illegible]

1875 Wt. W593/826 1,000,000 4/15 J.B.C. & A. A.D.S.S./Forms/C. 2118.

Appendix III

Copy

To:- Adjutant 172nd Bde R.F.A.

Report on the wire cutting carried out by 'A' 172nd Bde. on the 19th instant.

Battery Position B/183 about Q34 b. 3.5

Position of wire fired at Q 24 d 45 78

Observed from B/183 O.P. Q 29 c 05 05

Range 2625.

Names of Officers instructed — Lt G. Sanders and 2/Lt. Scott E.S.

Sd J. H. Sebag-Montefiore
OC A/172nd Bde

L.H.L.

Army Form C. 2118

Instructions regarding War Diaries and Intelligence Summaries are contained in F. S. Regs., Part II. and the Staff Manual respectively. Title Pages will be prepared in manuscript.

WAR DIARY
or
~~INTELLIGENCE~~ SUMMARY

(Erase heading not required.)

Place	Date	Hour	Summary of Events and Information	Remarks and references to Appendices
In the Field	26.4.16		Normal – weather fine & warm. "C" Battery carried out experiments with trench bridge. "B" Battery cut wire (Appendix IV)	[illegible]
	27.4.16		Fine & warm weather. Lt. Col. L. Esward DSO proceeded on leave to England.	[illegible]
	28.4.16 29.4.16 30.4.16		Weather fine. No particular incidents.	

1875 Wt. W593/826 1,000,000 4/15 J.B.C. & A. A.D.S.S./Forms/C. 2118.

Instructions regarding War Diaries and Intelligence Summaries are contained in F. S. Regs., Part II. and the Staff Manual respectively. Title Pages will be prepared in manuscript.

WAR DIARY
or
~~INTELLIGENCE SUMMARY~~
(Erase heading not required.)

172nd Bde RFA

XXXVI

Army Form C. 2118

Vol 6

Place	Date	Hour	Summary of Events and Information	Remarks and references to Appendices
Toutencourt	1.5.16 to 6.5.16		No particular incident. Weather fine. Lieut Col. L.E.S. Ward resumed command on return from leave 6.5.1916	[illegible]
	7.5.16		No events.	[illegible]
	8.5.16		Conference of Brigade Commanders at R.A.H.Q 4th Army Staff Ride. Weather showery and cold	[illegible]
	9.5.16		Weather fine No incidents	[illegible]
	10.5.16		Weather fine but dull No incidents.	[illegible]
	11.5.16		Weather fine. No incidents	[illegible]
	12.5.16		Weather overcast. No incidents	[illegible]
	13.5.16		Weather wet. No incidents	[illegible]
	14.5.16		Weather very wet. No incidents	[illegible]
	15.5.16		Weather very fine. No incidents	[illegible]
	16.5.16		Weather brilliantly fine. No incidents	[illegible]
	17.5.16		Weather fine. No incidents.	[illegible]
	18.5.16		Weather fine but dull. No incidents	[illegible]

1875 Wt. W593/826 1,000,000 4/15 J.B.C. & A. A.D.S.S./Forms/C. 2118.

Instructions regarding War Diaries and Intelligence Summaries are contained in F. S. Regs., Part II. and the Staff Manual respectively. Title Pages will be prepared in manuscript.

WAR DIARY
or
~~INTELLIGENCE~~ SUMMARY
(Erase heading not required.)

172nd Bde RFA

Army Form C. 2118

Place	Date	Hour	Summary of Events and Information	Remarks and references to Appendices
Forku contd	19.5.16		Lieut. Col. L.E.S. Ward resumed command of Brigade on return from leave of C.R.A. Weather fine & warm.	LLh
	20.5.16		Re-organization of Divisional artillery as follows:- Each 18pdr. Brigade to be composed of three 18pdr. batteries and one 4.5" Howitzer battery. Bde Amm Columns done away with and D.A.C. largely increased. This procedure was duly carried out.	LLh
			Lieut. H.E. Pitt appears in gazette as Captain. Weather fine & warm.	
	21.5.16		In accordance with re-organization scheme for Artillery D/172, Captain Gale ceased to belong to the Brigade, and was replaced by D/154 Howitzers under Capt. Newcombe. Weather fine & very warm	LLh
	22.5.16		C.O. visited forward gun positions at Thiepval & Hamel. Inspection of A B & C batteries in F.S. Marching order (dismounted). Weather fine in morning, but heavy rain during the afternoon & evening	LLh

Instructions regarding War Diaries and Intelligence Summaries are contained in F. S. Regs., Part II. and the Staff Manual respectively. Title Pages will be prepared in manuscript.

WAR DIARY
or
~~INTELLIGENCE~~ SUMMARY
(Erase heading not required.)

172nd Bde R.F.A

Army Form C. 2118

Place	Date	Hour	Summary of Events and Information	Remarks and references to Appendices
Forceville	23.5.16		Conference of Artillery Commanders at Bouzincourt. Trench Mortar Battery attached to the Brigade. Weather fine & a little cooler.	[illegible]
	24.5.16		Normal routine. Weather - colder, heavy rain began in the afternoon & continued all night.	[illegible]
	25.5.16		Normal routine. Weather fine but cold. No rain	[illegible]
	26.5.16		C.O inspected A B & C batteries in F.S Marching Order.	[illegible]
			Half holiday in commemoration of Bi-centenary of R.A. Weather - fine & warm.	[illegible]
	27.5.16		Visited wagon line of D Howitzer & inspected horses & harness. Also visited Mesnil & inspected work on group Communications. Weather fine & warm.	[illegible]
	28.5.16		Church Parade at Forceville. Weather fine & warm	[illegible]
	29.5.16		C.O. visited Artillery School at Havernas. Lieut E.G. Scott operated on for appendicitis. Moves of wagon lines cancelled. Weather fine but overcast. Rain during the night	[illegible] [illegible]
	30.5.16		Normal. Weather fine & warm	[illegible]

Instructions regarding War Diaries and Intelligence Summaries are contained in F. S. Regs., Part II. and the Staff Manual respectively. Title Pages will be prepared in manuscript.

WAR DIARY
or
~~INTELLIGENCE~~ SUMMARY
(Erase heading not required.)

172nd Bde R.F.A.

Army Form C. 2118

Place	Date	Hour	Summary of Events and Information	Remarks and references to Appendices
Tartincourt	31.5.16		Inspection of harness & appointments of Brigade Headquarters Capt J.H.K Lockhart joined the Brigade & was posted to C Battery Weather fine & warm	J.H.W.

1875 Wt. W593/826 1,000,000 4/15 J.B.C. & A. A.D.S.S./Forms/C. 2118.

Appendix II

To. Adjutant 172nd Bde RFA

Memo

I have to report, that as ordered I carried out an instructional wire cut yesterday.

Wire was cut at Q24d. 80.75

Climatic conditions were very bad. A gusty wind was a great disadvantage

Range was 4000, which I consider too long for effective cutting

Fuzes were bad throughout

Very little wire was cut.

50 rounds A.X. were fired

sd E.W. Bolitho Major
OC B 172nd Bde

12.4.1916

[illegible]

Appendix IV

Copy

Wire cutting by C/177th Bde
on the 26 4. 1916

Battery Position at Q34 d. 2.7
O.P. at Q23c. 8.2
Wire Cut at Q24d. 6.9
Range 2600 yards
Shrapnel with 80 fuzes
Small amount of wire cut
Officer under instruction Lt Wight
Useful instruction imparted

Sd. E W Bolitho Major RFA
OC C/177th Bde RFA

[illegible]

36th Divisional Artillery.

172nd BRIGADE.

ROYAL FIELD ARTILLERY.

JUNE 1916:

XXXVI

War Diary 172nd Bde RFA June 1916

VOL 7

Place	Date	Subject	Appendices
In the Field (Bertincourt)	June 1st 1916	Inspection of D Battery (Howitzer) in F. Marching order dismounted also inspected C Battery horses Weather fine and warm	[illegible]
	June 2nd	Reconnaissance in connection with the 4th Army Scheme carried out by C O & Battery Commanders of A B & D Batteries New orders for 4th Army Staff Ride received Weather fine & warm	[illegible]
	June 3rd	Inspection of A Battery F. marching order dismounted Inspection of Bde H2 F.S. marching order - mounted - all vehicles Weather fine & warm	[illegible]
	June 4th	Interviewed Gen Griffiths with reference to 4th Army Scheme Inspected special turn out of part of D Battery Weather cloudy - slight rain very cold	[illegible]
	June 5th	Work commenced on battery schemes in connection with 4th Army Staff Ride Practice for flag barrage for Infantry attack practised Weather cold with much rain	[illegible]
	June 6th	Work continued on battery schemes - maps & tracings completed ready for issue to BCs Weather cold & much rain	[illegible]
	June 7th	Further practice in flag barrage Adjutant proceeded to Hedauville to arrange battery areas in wood Conference of BCs of group in 4th Army Scheme - at which instructions with map tracings were issued for drawing up Battery schemes Weather wet & cold	[illegible]

War Diary 172nd Bde RFA June 1916

Place	Date	Subject	Appendices
In the Field (Forceville)	June 8th	Practice attack with flag barrage carried out. Flag barrage well and efficiently worked. Weather dull & overcast in the morning - rain in the afternoon. Temperature cold	[illegible]
	June 9th	Combined manoeuvres with 108th & 109th Infantry Bdes in Divisional training area. All batteries out. Scheme commenced at 9.30 am and continued till 2 pm. Weather fine & warm	[illegible]
	June 10th	Practice attack with flag barrage - orders for move of Brigade to Hedauville received. Weather atrocious, very wet & cold. Areas allotted to Batteries in the wood at Hedauville	[illegible]
	June 11th	Attended lecture at Senlis on battle of Jutland. Weather showery but warmer.	[illegible]
	June 12th	Brigade Headquarters moved to Hedauville with A Battery & camped in Hedauville Wood outskirts. Weather very wet & cold	[illegible]
	June 13th	B & C Batteries moved from Forceville to Hedauville Wood. Front scheme for 4th Army. Scheme sent into 36th Div RA HQ. Weather very wet & cold. Instructions received for Bde to go into action on the night 13-14th except 1 Section C Battery.	[illegible] [illegible]
	June 14th	C Battery moved into action. Revised group scheme sent into RA HQ. Weather overcast - windy & cold	[illegible]

War Diary 172nd Bde RFA June 1916

Place	Date	Subject	Appendices
Hedauville	June 15th	Whole Brigade in action Scheme for preliminary bombardment completed & issued to Batteries Weather wet and much rain	Llw
	June 16th	Scheme for intensive bombardment commenced Weather wet & rainy	Llw
	June 17th	Continued work on scheme Conference at RAHQ Weather fine & warmer	Llw
	June 18th	Scheme for intensive bombardment completed Weather fine & fairly warm	Llw
	June 19th	Operation temporarily postponed moved to Battle position near Mesnil Weather fine	Llw
Mesnil	June 20th	Raid scheme for W.X night completed ~~[illegible]~~ issued C Battery lost 3 men killed & one wounded in Hamel including Sr Wakeling Weather fine	Llw
	June 21st	Conference of Battery Commanders at Hedauville Visited Bde Commander 108th Bde at Varennes Communications completed & tested Weather fine	Llw
	June 22nd 3.35pm	Operations commenced at 9.30 am with wire cutting C/176 reports Ker OP in Jacobs Ladder put out of action by [illegible]	Llw

War Diary 172nd Bde R.F.A. June 1916

Place	Date	Subject	Appendices
Mesnil	June 22 5.40pm	Message from Div Arty Ropes tonight – written instructions for operation issued to all Batteries	LW
	5.50pm	Visited front OP & B/172 OP and inspected wire cut by A & B/172	LW
	6.40pm	Returned to front Report Centre	LW
	9. pm	Final instructions for Raid and Gas attack issued Zero 10pm	
	9.45pm	Reached front OP Gas operations commenced at 0.5 according to programme [illegible] Raid for operation was off (at 10.15)	LW
	10.45pm	Batteries instructed to carry on night tasks	LW
	22-23/6/16 night	After counter order of gas attack ordinary night tasks were carried out. Hostile fire on the whole was very slight	LW
	23.6.16	Operations commenced at dawn according to programme	LW
		Visited all OPs during the morning	LW
	12 noon	Casualties reported from A/172 1 man killed 3 men wounded	LW
	12.30pm	Test concentration on Crucifix Redoubt was carried out	LW

War Diary 172nd Bde RFA June 1916

Place	Date	Subject	Appendices
Mesnil	23.6.16	Considerable hostile fire very slight	Lw
	2 45 pm	Telephone instructions issued to put one Howitzer Battery on Thiepval Chateau. D/241 detailed reported in action at 3 27	Lw
	3 15 pm		
	6-7 pm	Making up reports	Lw
	6 40 pm	OC B/172 report pile of wire for repair purposes at Q24b 8 208	
		D/241 How instructed to dispose of it	Lw
	7 15 pm	OC D/241 reports having disposed of wire pile	Lw
	9.10 pm	Following important message received the use of ZEROIC oil in hydraulic buffers of your guns should cease Transmitted to BCs	Lw
	10 pm	Bde Major reports trench mortar active at R19c 1070 B/172 How detailed to deal with it	Lw
	10 25 pm	Capt Newcombe reports having blown up trench mortar bomb	Lw
	23/24.6.16 night	From 6 pm some increase in hostile fire Tasks according to programme	Lw
	11 pm	Code telegram concerning concentrated bombardment received	Lw
	24.6.16 6 10 am	Right group reports lachrymatory shells at Mesnil	Lw

~~Diary~~ 1/2nd Bde RFA June 1916

Place	Date	Subject	Appendices
Mesnil	24.6.16 7.30am	Fresh instructions for discharge of gas received. Operations commenced at dawn	Lw
	10 am	Conference of BCs on following points (a) Gas discharge (b) concentrated (c) Raid tonight	Lw
	11.45am	Orders received to put the batteries out of [illegible] ready to fire at any enemy driven out by Heavy Bombardment at 12 noon at same time Martinsart 1.30pm given by RA H2 [illegible] Batteries.	Lw
	12.5pm	Arrived at front OP	Lw
	1.23pm	2nd appeared to be making good practice on wire W of NEB.	Lw
	2.10pm	Message received Martinsart 2.30 Battalion Headquarters report much annoyance from 77 heavy stuff in Thiepval Wood	Lw
		Bde Major informed at [illegible] batteries put on	Lw
	2.30pm	Gas smoke from Thiepval. Enemy replied on E & NE face of Thiepval Wood chiefly with [illegible] gas [illegible] but not especially vigorous	Lw
	3.15pm	Impression. Smoke cloud very thin. Gas very local. Very little machine gun fire from enemy. Minimum of hostile artillery fire on our trenches in front line	Lw
	3.30pm	Very smoky in Ancre Valley between Mesnil [illegible]	Lw

War Diary 172nd Bde R.F.A. June 1916

Place	Date	Subject	Appendice
Mesnil	24.6.16 3.55pm	Steady fire by front. No hostile reply. N of Thiepval Wood	Lw
	4 pm	Light barrage N.E. of wood. Slight hostile barrage W face of Thiepval – all bursts of fire very high.	
	4.5 pm	Barrage extends towards Hamel (Shrapnel)	Lw
	4.10pm	Our fire quickens. Hostile barrage on W of wood bursting about 10 rds per minute	Lw
	4.18pm	Hostile barrage increased in intensity, to about 15 per minute. Impression: one or two batteries 77 only on this barrage 400 rds expended	
	4.30pm	front fire ceases	Lw
	4.35pm	Hostile barrage on W of Wood ceases. Impression: hostile fire heavy on Hamel & the Ancre Valley	Lw
	4.40pm	Batteries instructed to continue normal tasks	Lw
	5-8pm	Employed in routine office work	
	24-25.6.16 night 10.30pm	received telephone instructions from Bde Major for 2" How batteries to bombard P1 & support line. A Batteries notified by telephone	Lw
	10.45pm	arrived at front OP for Raid operation	Lw

War Diary 172nd Bde June 1916

Place	Date	Subject	Appendices
Mesnil	10.54 pm	Synchronised watches with Infantry	LW
	11.30 pm	Operation commenced	
	11.40	Infantry reported that they did not think 18 pdrs were working. Instructed batteries to quicken to 2 rds per gun per minute for 5 minutes.	LW
	12.20 pm	Informed by Infantry that they might be in hostile trenches for one hour. Instructed Batteries to keep steady rate of fire 1 rd per gun per minute until further orders	LW
	12.30 am	Communication with A15a broken. Re-established at 12.40 am. Hostile artillery fire slight	LW
	12.50 am	Infantry report having lost touch with raiding party. Batteries instructed to keep up same rate of fire	LW
	1.5 am	Hostile barrage on our front line N of Thiepval. Many red rockets going up from hostile trenches, chiefly from St Pierre Divion	LW
	1.16 am	Communication with TL broken (11th R I R)	LW
		Connection obtained through QB (108th Inf Bde)	LW
	1.20 am	Communication with CRA	LW
	1.25 am	Hostile barrage ceased about 10 mins previously	LW
	1.35 am	Instructions given to slow to 1 rd per 2 minute	LW

War Diary 172nd Bde RFA June 1916

Place	Date	Subject	Appendices
Mesnil	1.30 am	Infantry report raiding party in Sunken Road all batteries ceased fire & stand by.	LW
	2 am	Hostile barrage shell on	LW
	2.5 am	Batteries instructed to resume normal night tasks.	LW
	26.6.16	Operations commenced at 4.30 am in accordance with programme	LW
	12 noon	Instructions received for test concentration	LW
	4.30 pm	Returned from observation of test concentrations on R14 c & d & W face of Crucifix Redoubt	LW
	6 pm	Instructed to increase expenditure of ammunition on night tasks owing to reports of prisoners	LW
	9.30 pm	Damages to equipment serious 1 gun each A/172 B/172 & B/246	LW
	27.6.16	Very misty & difficult to see	LW
	10.15 am	Conference at H2 Right front	LW
	2 pm	Further alterations in tasks for intensive bombardment issued to B/246 A/172 & B/172	LW
	3.15 pm	Normal tasks proceeding	LW
	4.20 pm	Information received that 29th June is X Day. Batteries informed & instructed to carry on normal tasks. Casualties in Bde up to date: Killed 4 R.F.T. Wounded 1 off 10 R.F.A.	LW

War Diary 172nd Bde RFA June 1916

Place	Date	Subject	Appendices
Mesnil	27-28.6.16 night Normal	Normal tasks carried on	LW
	28.6.16 day	Another alteration to tasks for Z day received	LW
	12.15 pm	Made reconnaissance of front line wire & reported	LW
	2 pm	Normal programme proceeding.	LW
	5 pm	Verbal communication from OC 108th Inf Bde that he would	LW
	7.15 pm	like wire at Portadown cut. A/154 instructed to do so	LW
	29.6.16 day	arrived in OP at 8.11 am for bombardment operation	LW
	8.41 am	Hostile barrage on Thiepval commences ~~with~~	LW
	8.50 am	Hostile fire on Thiepval includes heavy howitzers at least two 15 cms	LW
	9.15 am	Very heavy shrapnel barrage on Ancre Road & Hamel	LW
		Retaliation on Hamel very heavy	LW
		on I.ns all firing short.	LW
	7.30 pm	Zero time received & issued to Batteries	LW
	11 pm	Batteries instructed to get [illegible] 100 rds per gun after 1 am	LW

War Diary 17th Bde June 1916

Place	Date	Subject	appendices
Mesnil	30.6.16	Reached O.P. very misty	LW
	6.35am	Hostile shrapnel barrage commences	LW
	6.40am	Hostile fire on Thiepval Wood increasing especially on NE face to E corner	LW
	6.49am	Hostile fire on Castor's post increases	LW
	6.50am	Smoke dust & our mist are practically preventing all observation	LW
		Fire on Hamel appears to be heavy	LW
	7.30am	Smoke discharge from Thiepval Wood. Hostile shrapnel barrage continues, bursts very high	LW
	7.15am	Hostile shrapnel barrage on Thiepval increases	LW
	7.20am	Our infantry leave our trenches	LW
	7.25am	Our Infantry massing in Sunken Road. No hostile barrage appears to be there. Heavy smoke barrage on left of attack	LW
	7.33am	Our infantry appear on hostile first line	LW
	7.40am	Hostile fire on Thiepval Wood very heavy	LW

War Diary 172nd Bde June 1916

Place	Date	Subject	Appendices
Mesnil	8 am	Our troops now appear to be occupying NW face of Crucifix Redoubt	LW
	8.5am	Enemy appear to be shelling their own 1st & 2nd Line. A	LW
	8.10am	Infantry advancing in support - attacking troops on crest in R19 c+d	LW
	8.15am	D/276 turned onto St Pierre Divion for 5 minutes on account of Infantry Report of machine guns	LW
	8.20am	Hostile barrage still heavy on Hamel	LW
	8.30am	Infantry report being held up at St Pierre Divion	LW
	8.45am	Message from Infantry. Stop Howitzers on St Pierre Divion. Battery D/276 informed	LW
	9am	Infantry report having reached C11 but are being held up by enfilade fire from C13 ([illegible])	LW
		Hostile fire on Hamel still heavy - intermittent on Thiepval	LW
	9.5am	Fire on Thiepval Wood increasing	LW
	9.15am	Hostile fire on Thiepval Wood & valley of the Ancre west of wood very heavy	LW

War Diary 172nd Bde June 1916

Place	Date	Subject	Appendices
Mesnil	9.40am	FOOs instructed to go forward to Crucifix Redoubt	Lw
		Infantry report Crucifix Redoubt now in our hands and	Lw
		advance being made on Beaucourt Station	Lw
	10.10am	Fire on Hamel lessening. Fire on Thiepval Wood N	Lw
		face diminishing	Lw
	10.45am	A/172 B/172 D/246 + D/172 ordered to be ready for	Lw
		counter attacks barrage on R 28 a c	Lw
		Enemy firing heavy shells on A line between A + NE	Lw
		face of Thiepval - also on Crucifix Redoubt - apparently	Lw
		3 heavy howitzers	Lw
	11 am	Shrapnel also now on Crucifix Redoubt	Lw
	11.40am	Shrapnel fire still on Beaumont Hamel	Lw
	12 noon	Shrapnel fire on Crucifix Redoubt diminishing; but	Lw
		increasing on Thiepval Wood N face	Lw
	12.30pm	Instruction from Bde Major to put two batteries on	Lw
		barrage on R 20 d + R 26 b A/154 + B/246 put on	Lw

War Diary 172nd Bde June 1916

Place	Date	Subject	Appx
Mesnil	12.35pm	Message from Adjutant to say counter attack from St Pierre Divion expected also machine gun at R19a 1050	Lw
		Section D/172 & Section B/246 put on with instructions to keep remainder of Battery in readiness A/172 also warned to be in readiness D/172 reports 1 gun put out of action.	Lw
	1 pm	General situation Crucifix Redoubt & part of C Line from C.H. towards C.12 in our hands. St Pierre Divion & B [illegible] held by enemy. Counter attack from this point expected	Lw
	1-2 pm	Busy with orders to Batteries.	Lw
	2 pm	Hostile fire on Crucifix Redoubt & Hamel diminished	Lw
	6.30 pm	Situation our troops still holding part of Crucifix Redoubt B Line to rear B19 & A Line at ~~[illegible]~~ 24 d 8070 about	Lw
	7.15 pm	Enemy infantry seen in R14 B/246 & A/172 opened fire on them	Lw
	7.25 pm	Enemy again advancing from R14	Lw
	7.30 pm	our infantry retiring	Lw
	8.25 pm	Enemy shelling this point heavily	Lw

36th Divisional Artillery.

<u>172nd BRIGADE</u>.

<u>ROYAL FIELD ARTILLERY</u>.

<u>J U L Y 1 9 1 6</u>:

36 July Vol 8

Army Form C. 2118.

WAR DIARY
or
INTELLIGENCE SUMMARY

(Erase heading not required.)

Instructions regarding War Diaries and Intelligence Summaries are contained in F. S. Regs., Part II. and the Staff Manual respectively. Title Pages will be prepared in manuscript.

172nd Bde RFA.

Place	Date	Hour	Summary of Events and Information	Remarks and references to Appendices
Mesnil.	1-2.7.16	1. am	Situation. - Our troops still appear to be holding part of Crucifix Redoubt, part of A & B & C. Lines, but in a very precarious state as their flanks are uncovered. Our casualties are very heavy. Night barrage established.	
		1.30. am	Instruction received through adjutant that three Battalions would attack at dawn.	
	2.7.16	4.30 am	at O.P.	
		7.30 am	no sign of our attack	
		9. am	Our infantry reported at B.17. B19. in the NEB & South of it	
		10 am	no change in situation. Enemy has been firing a few rounds of shrapnel on his own line about the NEB.	
		10.25 am	Informed of decision to re-inforce troops in German lines	
		10.35 am	A knot of 5 or 6 of our men seen at A.19 sitting on parapet. Also two men moving about at Q24 d. 40.80.	
		12.5 pm	We appear to be dropping shells on B Line in neighbourhood of [illegible]. During last hour enemy have dropped a few heavy shells in burst on Thiepval Wood.	

2449 Wt. W14957/M90 750,000 1/16 J.B.C. & A. Forms/C.2118/12.

Army Form C. 2118.

WAR DIARY
or
~~INTELLIGENCE~~ SUMMARY

(Erase heading not required.)

Instructions regarding War Diaries and Intelligence Summaries are contained in F. S. Regs., Part II. and the Staff Manual respectively. Title Pages will be prepared in manuscript.

Place	Date	Hour	Summary of Events and Information	Remarks and references to Appendices
Mesnil	2.7.16	12.5 pm	Our Infantry seen moving about A lines & up communication trench towards [illegible]. They appear to be attempting to block the trenches between enemy and themselves by use of explosives	[illegible]
		2.15 pm to 2.20 pm	[illegible] at intensive rates of bombardment.	
		2.30 pm	First party of Infantry re-inforcements all in.	
		2.45 pm	Hostile barrage between A line and our trenches very heavy.	
		4.10 pm	Fire reduced to 1 round per gun per minute. Communication with C/172 has been broken for some hours.	
		5.40 pm	appearance of hostile counter attack from W. face of Fort Schwaben. A/172 & B/172 put on.	
		5.50 pm	Fire slowed down, and aerial reconnaissance asked for. B/246 C/246 & A/154 ordered to cease fire for 30 minutes	
		6. pm	East face of Thiepval heavily shelled.	
		6.30 pm	Communications with C/172 re-established	
		7.30 pm	Enemy counter attack worked up communication trenches & B line from St. Pierre Divion. C/172 & A/154 took them in enfilade & remaining batteries joined in. This counter attack was completely crushed the enemy flying to St. Pierre Divion.	

Instructions regarding War Diaries and Intelligence Summaries are contained in F. S. Regs., Part II. and the Staff Manual respectively. Title Pages will be prepared in manuscript.

WAR DIARY
or
~~INTELLIGENCE~~ SUMMARY
(Erase heading not required.)

Army Form C. 2118.

Place	Date	Hour	Summary of Events and Information	Remarks and references to Appendices
Mesnil	2-3.7.16		To R.A. H.Q. for Conference, returning to O.P. at 12.30 am.	
			S.O.S. call given between 2.25 + 2.30.	
			All guns opened rapid fire which was stopped after a few minutes as it was considered that it was not serious.	
			S.O.S. purely imaginary	
	3.7.16		General situation – our troops holding front line A and support line A from A.14 to A.19 and on the NEB.	[illegible]
			Morning quiet but much confusion owing to bad communications and panic S.O.S. calls.	
			Group came under 49th Div. tactically from 7 pm 2nd July.	
			Small hostile movements about St. Pierre Divion and Crows[?].	
			Our infantry report being in possession of A.19 which they are consolidating.	
		5.15 pm	18 pdr. Batteries standing by and firing when targets appear. Howitzers keeping up slow rate of fire. Shell fire on Thiepval Wood. N.E. Corner very heavy + North face has been very much knocked about.	
		5.30 pm	At O.P. situation quite quiet.	
		8. pm	Batteries switched to night barrage.	

Army Form [illegible]. 2118.

Instructions regarding War Diaries and Intelligence Summaries are contained in F. S. Regs., Part II. and the Staff Manual respectively. Title Pages will be prepared in manuscript.

WAR DIARY
or
~~INTELLIGENCE SUMMARY~~
(Erase heading not required.)

Place	Date	Hour	Summary of Events and Information	Remarks and references to Appendices
Mesnil	3.7.16	9.40 pm	Orders & instructions for work in future. Operation orders issued to all Batteries. Scrap on night barrage points	
		10.30 pm	Instructions from Bde Major 49th Div. that infantry patrols were going out to B line – barrage lifted off St. Pierre Divion and all communication trenches & placed beyond B Line.	
	4.7.16		One S.O.S. Call during the night	
		9. am	Proceeded to 148th Bde HQ. Thiepval for Conference on projected night operation	
		2.30 pm	Hostile attack on captured German trenches reported in midst of storm. All Batteries to barrage front of our position. Attack repulsed.	
		7.30 pm	Operation orders issued	
			<u>General</u> Refitting reorganization of communication taken in hand. Weather atrocious	
	4-5.7.16	1.45 am	Get into communication with Infantry.	
		2. am	Operation commences.	
		2.50 am	Information received that first attack had failed. Batteries instructed to stand by until 4. am when 2nd attack would take place	

2449 Wt. W14957/M90 750,000 1/16 J.B.C. & A. Forms/C.2118/12.

Army Form C. 2118.

Instructions regarding War Diaries and Intelligence Summaries are contained in F. S. Regs., Part II. and the Staff Manual respectively. Title Pages will be prepared in manuscript.

WAR DIARY
or
~~INTELLIGENCE SUMMARY~~
(Erase heading not required.)

Place	Date	Hour	Summary of Events and Information	Remarks and references to Appendices
Mesnil	4-5.7.16	4. am	Second attack commences.	
	5.7.16	5.5 am	B/172 reports fighting at A.19 & that our troops appear to have reached a point about ½ way between A.18 & A.20.	
		8. am	Reports of hostile concentrations about St. Pierre Divion & R.20.a received from various sources.	
		10.am	Situation declares itself as a definite bombing attack on the left flank of captured trenches. Batteries brought into action D/172 D/246 B & C/172 A/154 Two batteries left front, one 6" How. & one 8" How. also assisted in repelling his attack. Situation did not develop in R.20.a.	
		12.15 pm	Situation about St. Pierre Divion well in hand. Afternoon – quiet and normal.	
		7 pm	Instructed to take over defence of part of 29th Div. front. Following batteries tactically in front:- Left Bank of Ancre A.173. C/173. Bullock's Battery 1 section D/172.	

2449 Wt. W14957/M90 750,000 1/16 J.B.C. & A. Forms/C.2118/12.

Army Form C. 2118.

Instructions regarding War Diaries and Intelligence Summaries are contained in F. S. Regs., Part II. and the Staff Manual respectively. Title Pages will be prepared in manuscript.

WAR DIARY
or
~~INTELLIGENCE~~ SUMMARY
(Erase heading not required.)

Place	Date	Hour	Summary of Events and Information	Remarks and references to Appendices
Mesnil	5.7.16	7 pm	Right bank of Ancre. D/246. B/246. C/246. A/172. B/172. C/172. A/154. on left bank	
			night 5th 6th Very quiet.	
	6.7.16		Intimation received that bombing operation proposed for yesterday would be carried on today.	
		2. pm	Operation order issued for bombing attack.	
		2.30 pm	Enemy about 300 strong reported moving into trenches about B.15. (Aeroplanes).	
			Enemy reported moving into 'D' line through R14 b+d.	
			a few enemy reported in the vicinity of A.19.	
		3. pm	Following batteries in action	
			B/246, C/246, D/246 } B.15 etc	
			A/154 } on R19 b+d	
			B/172, C/172 } on trenches about St Pierre Divion	

2449 Wt. W14957/M90 750,000 1/16 J.B.C. & A. Forms/C.2118/12.

Army Form C. 2118.

Instructions regarding War Diaries and Intelligence Summaries are contained in F. S. Regs., Part II. and the Staff Manual respectively. Title Pages will be prepared in manuscript.

WAR DIARY
or
~~INTELLIGENCE SUMMARY~~
(Erase heading not required.)

Place	Date	Hour	Summary of Events and Information	Remarks and references to Appendices
Mesnil	7.7.16	1.30 am	Operation orders received, framed & issued to batteries	38
		2.am	First S.O.S. call from the Infantry.	
			Subsequent very heavy shelling of Thiepval Wood.	
		4.am	S.O.S from Thiepval Wood.	
		7.30 am	Infantry report having now withdrawn from the captured trenches and being in occupation of our original first line.	
		9.20 am	Situation appears to be somewhat easier. Heavy smoke barrage reported	
		9.30 am	Batteries ~~[illegible]~~ instructed to cease fire, section at a time, to cool guns. F.O.O. reports our fire falling short, just in front of our own trenches.	
		9.45 am	All batteries ordered to make up to 350 rounds per gun including usual percentage of H.E.	
		9.50 am.	Hostile fire Thiepval Wood reported as practically ceased.	
		10.am	Saw Major Bullock and arranged times of fire for B/248	
		10.15 am	During the operation the fire on Hamel usually very heavy was reported as slight.	
		11.am	No change in the situation. Enemy reported to be using Curve trench freely.	

2449 Wt. W14957/M90 750,000 1/16 J.B.C. & A. Forms/C.2118/12.

Army Form C. 2118.

Instructions regarding War Diaries and Intelligence Summaries are contained in F. S. Regs., Part II. and the Staff Manual respectively. Title Pages will be prepared in manuscript.

WAR DIARY
or
~~INTELLIGENCE SUMMARY~~
(Erase heading not required.)

Place	Date	Hour	Summary of Events and Information	Remarks and references to Appendices
Mesnil	7.7.16	11.30 am.	Distribution of fire	
			B/246 - R 19c 8030 - A.15	
			C/246 - A 15 - R 19c 4050.	
			A/172 - R 19c 4050 - Q 24 d. 8060	
			B/172 - Q 24 d. 8060 - Sunken Road. Q 24 d. 4070.	
			B/248 - Zig Zag trench + St Pierre Divion	
			A/154 - Enfilade 1st and support line A	
			C/172 - Curve trench approaches to St. Pierre Divion + enfilade of 1st + support line A	
			D/172 - Curve trench and 1st + 2nd line A + communication trenches to River Ancre.	
			D/246. (Machine guns at A.18 and A.15 special task) 1st + 2nd line A. + communication trenches as far N as Q 24 d. 9070.	
		11.45 am.	Hostile fire Thiepval practically ceased.	
		2 pm	Situation unchanged. Enemy shelling Mesnil + Battery positions Information received that we had captured Contalmaison - Ovillers, La Boiselle + Mametz Wood.	

2449 Wt. W14957/M90 750,000 1/16 J.B.C. & A. Forms/C.2118/12.

Army Form C. 2118.

Instructions regarding War Diaries and Intelligence Summaries are contained in F. S. Regs., Part II. and the Staff Manual respectively. Title Pages will be prepared in manuscript.

WAR DIARY
or
~~INTELLIGENCE SUMMARY~~
(Erase heading not required.)

Place	Date	Hour	Summary of Events and Information	Remarks and references to Appendices
Mesnil	7.7.16	4.30 pm	Situation unchanged. Enemy shelling battery positions	38
		8 pm	Orders for night barrage issued - allowance for night ~~barrage~~ firing 80 rounds. Situation quiet.	
		9 pm	Situation unchanged	
	7-8.7.16		Quiet night - one call for retaliation	
	8.7.16	11. am	Enemy's red-cross parties reported collecting on battlefield matter referred to the 49th Division. Instructions received to fire over them as a warning, and if they continue are to be fired on.	
			from Casualties up to date.	
			Officers 1 killed 4 wounded	
			R+F. 3 do. 28 "	
			1 Missing	
		11.15 am.	Instructions received not to fire on Red Cross.	
		11.30 am.	Lieut. Freeman reported killed (by 21 centimetre) at Hamel.	
		2 pm	Considerable movement in enemy trenches reported from A.15 to neighbourhood of B.15. Howitzer + enfilade battery put on All guns in action except one each in D/172 + A/154. + one in C/172	

2449 Wt. W14957/M90 750,000 1/16 J.B.C. & A. Forms/C.2118/12.

Army Form C. 2118.

Instructions regarding War Diaries and Intelligence Summaries are contained in F. S. Regs., Part II. and the Staff Manual respectively. Title Pages will be prepared in manuscript.

WAR DIARY
or
~~INTELLIGENCE~~ SUMMARY
(Erase heading not required.)

Place	Date	Hour	Summary of Events and Information	Remarks and references to Appendices
Mesnil	8.7.16	8 pm	Instructions received not to fire while British Red Cross are out. Batteries informed	
		10.5 pm	Personally tested communications with Infantry.	
	9.7.16		A quiet night.	
			C/172 two guns - withdrawn from Hamel to C/154 position	
			All guns in action except one in A/154.	
		5.10 pm	Orders for demonstration received & issued to A/154. A/172. B/172. D/172 B/246.	
		5.50 pm	Operation completed. Enemy retaliated on Thiepval Wood.	
		6.10 pm	Following relief in progress A/154 by A/248 Capt. Lupton B/172 " C/248 " Fowler. C/172 " B/247 " Durst.	
		7. pm	B/247 night barrage ~~A/154~~ A.15 to the NEB.	
			A quiet night.	

2449 Wt. W14957/M90 750,000 1/16 J.B.C. & A. Forms/C.2118/12.

Army Form C. 2118.

Instructions regarding War Diaries and Intelligence Summaries are contained in F. S. Regs., Part II. and the Staff Manual respectively. Title Pages will be prepared in manuscript.

WAR DIARY
or
~~INTELLIGENCE SUMMARY~~
(Erase heading not required.)

Place	Date	Hour	Summary of Events and Information	Remarks and references to Appendices
Mesnil	10.7.16	a.m.	Very quiet day	
		4 pm	Instructions received to repeat demonstration of yesterday Following batteries instructed A.172. D/172. D/246 A.248. & C/248	
	11.7.16		Quiet night.	
		4.30 pm	Information received that the remaining batteries and Bde H.Q. are to be relieved.	
		11. pm	1 Section A/172 & D/172 withdrawn from action & proceed to wagon lines.	
	12.7.16		A quiet night.	
		1. pm	Colonel Whitley 246th Bde arrived to take over command of group	
		1.30 pm	Enemy began to shell battery opposite H.Q. dug-out	
		4. pm	Corporal Hammond killed. Gunner Faulkner, my servant wounded slightly.	
		5.50 pm	Handed over command of group to Col. Whitley.	

2449 Wt. W14957/M90 750,000 1/16 J.B.C. & A. Forms/C.2118/12.

Army Form C. 2118.

Instructions regarding War Diaries and Intelligence Summaries are contained in F. S. Regs., Part II. and the Staff Manual respectively. Title Pages will be prepared in manuscript.

WAR DIARY
or
~~INTELLIGENCE SUMMARY~~

(Erase heading not required.)

Place	Date	Hour	Summary of Events and Information	Remarks and references to Appendices
Mesnil	12.7.16	7.30 pm	Arrived at Hedauville Brigade is following state A & D Batteries - complete B & C do no guns. March orders issued.	
	13.7.16		Move postponed. Brigade remained at Hedauville	
	14.7.16		Brigade marched from Hedauville to Franches, about 20 miles	
	15.7.16		Franches to Fillievre, about 15 miles	
	16.7.16		Marched from Fillievre to Berguenuse - about 16 miles. Weather fine & warm.	
	17.7.16		Marched from Berguenuse to Clarques - about 14 miles. Weather fine & warm except for some slight drizzle in the morning.	
	18.7.16		Marched from Clarques to Nordausque - passing through St. Omer. about 20 miles. Brigade billeted at Nordausque. Gun state of Brigade A & D batteries complete. B battery has 3 guns but no sights. Weather - some drizzle in the morning but fine & warm afterwards.	

2449 Wt. W14957/M90 750,000 1/16 J.B.C. & A. Forms/C.2118/12.

Instructions regarding War Diaries and Intelligence Summaries are contained in F. S. Regs., Part II. and the Staff Manual respectively. Title Pages will be prepared in manuscript.

WAR DIARY

or

~~INTELLIGENCE SUMMARY~~

(Erase heading not required.)

Army Form C. 2118.

Place	Date	Hour	Summary of Events and Information	Remarks and references to Appendices
Nordausque	19.7.16		Brigade in Billets at Nordausque.	
		2.40 pm	Instructions received to march to St. Omer. Brigade billeted at Arques.	
	20.7.16		Brigade marched to Moolenacker. Orders received to take over portion of line held by Centre Group 24th Division. Weather fine & warm.	
	21.7.16		BCs went forward to take over battery positions in new area. Batteries arrived on wagon lines at 6 pm. Relief to be carried out during the night. Guns taken over as follows:-	
			B/172 four guns complete from C/154	
			C/172 } Two new guns from Ordnance } two guns complete from B/154	
			Night quiet	
	22.7.16		Relief reported complete at 6 am. Visits from Divisional Commander 70th Division & C.R.A. 50th Div. Visited battery positions of A/154 and C/172. During the afternoon accompanied Generals Brock & Philpot in a reconnaissance. Weather fine & warm.	

2449 Wt. W14957/M90 750,000 1/16 J.B.C. & A. Forms/C.2118/12.

Army Form C. 2118.

Instructions regarding War Diaries and Intelligence Summaries are contained in F. S. Regs., Part II. and the Staff Manual respectively. Title Pages will be prepared in manuscript.

WAR DIARY
or
~~INTELLIGENCE SUMMARY~~

(Erase heading not required.)

Place	Date	Hour	Summary of Events and Information	Remarks and references to Appendices
Neuve-Eglise	23.7.16		Interviewed Brig. Gen. Clifford commanding 149th Inf. Bde. Visited battery positions & O.Ps of A/172, B/172 & D/172 & wagon line of B/172. Information received that Major A.D. Murray was posted to 33rd Division as a Brigade Commander. Informed by Bde. Major 36th Div. that I had no command of T.Ms. Weather fine & warm	
	24.7.16		Morning spent in revision of all Operation & Communications Orders for the Group. Batteries continued their registration. Weather - overcast but warm & no rain	
	25.7.16		CRA 50th Division visited Group Headquarters. Notification received of certain changes to take place in present dispositions. Weather - as yesterday.	
	26.7.16		Following alterations took place in Group. A/172 & B/172 passed to tactical command of Right Group. A/173 came into Group tactically from Left Group. Carried out reconnaissance of proposed battery positions. About 10.pm "A gas alarm" was given from the South. Weather dull but warm.	

2449 Wt. W14957/M90 750,000 1/16 J.B.C. & A. Forms/C.2118/12.

Instructions regarding War Diaries and Intelligence Summaries are contained in F. S. Regs., Part II. and the Staff Manual respectively. Title Pages will be prepared in manuscript.

WAR DIARY

or

~~INTELLIGENCE~~ SUMMARY

(Erase heading not required.)

Army Form C. 2118.

Place	Date	Hour	Summary of Events and Information	Remarks and references to Appendices
Neuve-Eglise	27.7.16		Day spent in Office Work. Reconnaissance of proposed battery positions carried out by Capt Gale & Lt. Simpson. All orders for new distribution of group brought up to date. Weather cloudy but warm	
	28.7.16		Fake gas alarm during the night. Instructions received that the group H2 was to move to Dranoutre & would be relieved on 30/31st & 31st/1st.	
			Weather fine & warm. An aerial Combat took place about 5 pm in neighbourhood of group H2.	
	29.7.16		Work on 2nd Army Scheme commenced. Group H2 moved to Dranoutre. Weather fine & warm.	
	30.7.16		At Dranoutre Instructions received from 50th Division & 36th Div. with reference to handing over. Weather fine - warm - very sunny	
	31.7.16		Handed over command of group & returned to Neuve Eglise. Work on 2nd Army Scheme gun positions stopped. Weather fine & warm	

2449 Wt. W14957/M90 750,000 1/16 J.B.C. & A. Forms/C.2118/12.

Instructions regarding War Diaries and Intelligence Summaries are contained in F. S. Regs., Part II. and the Staff Manual respectively. Title Pages will be prepared in manuscript.

WAR DIARY
or
~~INTELLIGENCE~~ SUMMARY
(Erase heading not required.)

August 1916 — 172nd Bde R.F.A.

Army Form C. 2118.

Vol 9

Place	Date	Hour	Summary of Events and Information	Remarks and references to Appendices
In the Field	1.8.16		Distribution of Brigade. A & B batteries attached to left group. D. Battery attached to Right Group. C Battery not in action. Bde. H.Q. not in action. Inspected harness of Bde H.Q. Weather fine and hot.	[initials]
	2.8.16		Quiet day. Fine and hot. Visited O.P.s on Hill 63.	[initials]
	3.8.16		Carried out reconnaissance for Defence scheme G.H.Q. 2 line. Weather fine & hot. Enemy's gun fire slight but much trench mortar activity.	[initials]
	4.8.16		Instructions received that a new (left) group was to be formed to consist of 172nd Bde & A.154. Weather fine & hot.	[initials]
	5.8.16		One section A.154 & C/172 moved into action in connection with the new left group. Visited battery position of A.154 & made small reconnaissance for new position of C/172. The communications of C/172 are very unsatisfactory. Weather hot and fine. Operation order No. 1. (appendix 1.)	[initials]
	6.8.16		Visited A & B battery gun positions and also saw the O.C. 107th Inf Bde. Weather fine & warm but cooler than previous days. Hostile Artillery quiet.	[initials]
	7.8.16		Accompanied C.R.A. 36th Division in visit to the four 18 pdr battery positions of the group.	[initials]
		5.30 pm	At 5.30 pm Infantry requested heavy retaliation for trenches C.3 & C.4. "Factory" retaliation ordered to commence at 5.45 pm. Rate of fire ordered 1 rd per gun per minute for 10 minutes. 2 rds per gun per minute for 5 minutes and return to first rate for last five minutes – i.e. 25 rds per gun for a period of 20 minutes.	
		5.55 pm	Infantry report retaliation as sufficient. Intimation received that C/172 would go into their original position.	
	8.8.16		Visited Battalion Hd. Qrs. of both sectors & Company H.Q. of Right Sector. In the evening visited C Battery Wagon line at Dranoutre. At 3 pm infantry rang up for retaliation for D.1 & D.2 "Cross Roads" retaliation put on at 3.10 pm. Infantry report result satisfactory. 1 section C/172 went into action in their original position. A quiet night – weather fine & very hot. Operation order No. 2 issued (appendix II)	[initials]

2449 Wt. W14957/M90 750,000 1/16 J.B.C. & A. Forms/C.2118/12.

Instructions regarding War Diaries and Intelligence Summaries are contained in F. S. Regs., Part II. and the Staff Manual respectively. Title Pages will be prepared in manuscript.

WAR DIARY
or
~~INTELLIGENCE~~ SUMMARY

(Erase heading not required.)

Army Form C. 2118.

Place	Date	Hour	Summary of Events and Information	Remarks and references to Appendices
In the Field	9.8.16.		Visited OPs A & B Batteries and saw guns fired on S.O.S points. Tracing of front trench map completed.	[signature]
		3.15pm 3.30pm	Infantry called for strong retaliation. ~~3.30pm~~ "Ontario" retaliation was applied. Night quiet. Weather fine & very hot. Visited D Battery wagon line.	[signature]
	10.8.16		Visited Battalion Headquarters & Company Hd Qrs in left Sector. Saw S.O.S points fired on by A 154 & C/172. Retaliation for Tm's was called for about 4.30pm. Weather fine & hot. Night quiet	[signature]
	11.8.16		Visited C Battery gun position and saw new billets & accommodation. Visited A Battery wagon line & inspected all buildings, accommodation & horses. Weather hot & fine.	
	12.8.16		Continued trouble with communications to A.154 & C/172. Visited Right Sub Sector Bn. H.Q. at MacBrides Mansions saw Bn Commander & two Coy. Cos. Hostile trench mortars opened fire as usual about 3.30pm. A combined retaliation with H.A group applied at N.36.d.2080 – N.36.d 36. Weather fine & very hot.	[signature]
	13.8.16		Morning quiet. Enemy Tm's were active in the afternoon & usual retaliation was carried out.	[signature]
		7.pm	At 7pm a combined retaliation (18 pdrs & 6" Howitzers) was made on front line enemy trench in N 36 d. with good results. Inspected wagon line of B/172. Weather overcast & cooler.	
	14.8.16		Carried out preliminary reconnaissance for guns for close defence of Hill 63. Visited Company H.Q. in diagonal and C2 trenches & tested battery communication at OK point. Visited OPs of A. B & D/172 with C.R.A. Communications working better on the whole. Weather overcast – some rain – still very warm. (Precis of Arrangements LEFT GROUP) Appendix III	[signature]
	~~12.8.16~~		~~Continued trouble with communications to A.154 & C/172. Visited Right Sub Sector Bn. H.Q. at MacBrides Mansions saw Bn Commander & two Coy. Cos. Hostile trench mortars opened fire as usual about 3.30pm. A combined retaliation with HA group applied at N.36.d.2080 – N.36.d.36~~	

2449 Wt. W14957/M90 750,000 1/16 J.B.C. & A. Forms/C.2118/12.

Instructions regarding War Diaries and Intelligence Summaries are contained in F. S. Regs., Part II. and the Staff Manual respectively. Title Pages will be prepared in manuscript.

WAR DIARY
or
~~INTELLIGENCE~~ SUMMARY
(Erase heading not required.)

Army Form C. 2118.

Place	Date	Hour	Summary of Events and Information	Remarks and references to Appendices
In the Field	15.8.16		A very quiet night. Carried out final reconnaissance for guns for defence of Hill 63. Inspected wagon lines of Bde H.Q. & C/172. There has been no trench mortar attack by enemy for two days. Weather - some showers - cooler - strong west wind all day.	[illegible]
	16.8.16		Very quiet night. Visited Brig. Gen. 107th Inf. Bde & discussed question of retaliation with him. A/172 reported about 2 pm that heavy shelling was going on in their neighbourhood. They reported to same effect about 4.45 pm. The Brig. Major was asked for retaliation by H.A. front. Considerable trouble over communications with A/154 & C/172 batteries. Weather - cloudy but no rain - very close	
	17.8.16		A quiet night. Visited battalion H.Q. of Right & Left Sectors & both Company Headquarters of Left Sector. Communications A/154 & C/172 finally adjusted. Weather showery & close	[illegible]
	18.8.16		Night quiet. About 3.15 pm B Battery report one man wounded shell fire. Operation order No. 3 issued for bombardment of Middle Farm & Four Huns Farm on 19th (appendix IV). Weather - fine - no rain - temperature cool.	[illegible]
	19.8.16		Night quiet. Operation order No. 3 cancelled. Operation order (modified) ordered by CRA	[illegible]
		3.30 pm	Hostile T.M.'s became very active - retaliation given at once.	
		6.30 pm	A retaliation with 18 pdrs & 6" Hows. carried out on hostile front line near Factory Farm.	
	20.8.16		Night quiet. An unusually quiet day. Visited wagon lines of A & D Batteries. Lt. H.R.J. Furness rejoined from England. Weather showery - but warm. Capt J.F.K. Lockhart transferred to 173 Bde vice Capt. A.E. Pitt posted to 172nd Bde	[illegible]
	21.8.16		A good deal of rifle & machine gun fire during the night but Artillery both sides very quiet. Orders for "defence scheme" got out (appendix V). M.G.R.A. General Franks inspected the battery positions of A.B. & D Batts. About 4 pm Hostile T.M.'s became active - retaliation was at once applied. Inspected wagon lines of Bde H.Q. Weather cloudy - close - occasional small showers.	[illegible]

2449 Wt. W14957/M90 750,000 1/16 J.B.C. & A. Forms/C.2118/12.

Instructions regarding War Diaries and Intelligence Summaries are contained in F. S. Regs., Part II. and the Staff Manual respectively. Title Pages will be prepared in manuscript.

Army Form C. 2118.

WAR DIARY
or
~~INTELLIGENCE SUMMARY~~

(Erase heading not required.)

Place	Date	Hour	Summary of Events and Information	Remarks and references to Appendices
In the Field	22.8.16		Usual rifle fire & machine gun fire. Visited Battalion Headquarters of both right & left sectors. Enemy was shelling Neuve Eglise – Wulverghem Road. Inspected battery position A & B batteries. About 5.30 pm hostile TMs & Artillery opened fire. Front at once retaliated. Weather fine & hot. Gas alert given at 6 pm.	[illegible]
	23.8.16		Visited battery position C/172 & A.154 during the morning. Enemy quiet – no trench mortars. Visited wagon line B/172 & the Bde Gen. 107th Inf Bde. Weather fine & warm.	[illegible]
	24.8.16		night quiet. Inspected battery positions A/172 & B/172 with a view to their being converted into 6 gun battery positions. Enemy's TMs busy on trenches D.1 & D.2 about 3.45 pm. Batteries gave local retaliation & howitzers also fired on both sectors. An operation (Operation Order 3) (Appendix VI) was undertaken in the evening as a return of TMs	[illegible]
	25.8.16		night quiet. Infantry relief carried out. At B Battery gun position during the morning. Inspected wagon line C/172 in the afternoon. Very little hostile activity during the day. Weather overcast & dull – very close.	[illegible]
	26.8.16		Machine guns active during the night. Visited C battery gun position & saw site for two new gun pits. Consulted OC 107th Inf Bde on subject point for raid. Weather wet during morning & very close.	[illegible]
	27.8.16		Very quiet during night. About 9.30 am enemy showed some activity (artillery) on trench C.4. – C/172 gave retaliation. Accompanied Brig Gen. 107th Inf Bde to O.Ps. B & D Batts. Inspected wagon lines A & D Batts. Weather showery & warm. Strong west wind.	[illegible]

2449 Wt. W14957/M90 750,000 1/16 J.B.C. & A. Forms/C.2118/12.

Instructions regarding War Diaries and Intelligence Summaries are contained in F. S. Regs., Part II. and the Staff Manual respectively. Title Pages will be prepared in manuscript.

WAR DIARY

or

~~INTELLIGENCE~~ SUMMARY

(Erase heading not required.)

Army Form C. 2118.

Place	Date	Hour	Summary of Events and Information	Remarks and references to Appendices
In the field	28.8.16		A quiet night. Interviewed O.C. 107th Infantry Bde on subject of raid. Visited Company HQ in trenches C2, 3, 4 & D.1 & D2 & tested the communications of A.C/172 & A.154. Also visited both battalion HQ. Hostile artillery & T.Ms active about 12.45. We retaliated over C.3. Operation orders No.4. issued (appendix VII) Weather showery, hot & close - windy	[signature]
	29.8.16		Night quiet. Conference of group commanders at Centre group. Operation orders No.5 issued (appendix VIII). Gas alert ordered at 12 noon. Operations cancelled at 9.30pm. Weather wet, with wind from N.E. to E. a heavy thunder storm about 3pm. Appendix 1 to left group O.O. No 4 issued (appendix IX).	[signature]
	30.8.16		Night quiet. Morning spent in completing Defence Scheme. A wet afternoon. Night 30th/31st. 11.5pm telephone message received that operations vide O.O. 5 & 4 would take place.	[signature]
		11.30pm	Written messages sent to batteries informing them that operations would take place and giving time	[signature]
		1.34am	Operation commenced.	[signature]
		1.45am	Informed by Bde Major 107th Inf. Bde that no gas had been discharged.	
		2.4am	Operation closed.	[signature]
		2.10am	Operation order No.4 cancelled. Batteries directed to resume normal night line. Appendix 1a to O.O. No.4 issued (appendix X)	

2449 Wt. W14957/M90 750,000 1/16 J.B.C. & A. Forms/C.2118/12.

Instructions regarding War Diaries and Intelligence Summaries are contained in F. S. Regs., Part II. and the Staff Manual respectively. Title Pages will be prepared in manuscript.

WAR DIARY
or
~~INTELLIGENCE SUMMARY~~
(Erase heading not required.)

Army Form C. 2118.

Place	Date	Hour	Summary of Events and Information	Remarks and references to Appendices
In the Field	31.8.16		Visited battery position of A. B. & C/172 & A.154 during the morning & afternoon. Orders received that operations would be carried out as for night of 30/31st. Batteries informed. At 1.30 a.m. 31st/1st cancelled operations on receipt of information from the trenches. Weather fine, fresh & warm.	[illegible]

2449 Wt. W14957/M90 750,000 1/16 J.B.C. & A. Forms/C.2118/12.

C O P Y.

Operation Orders No.1.

By

Lieut. Col. L.E.S.Ward, D.S.O., R.F.A.

Commanding Left Group.

appendix I

Ref. Map. Wytschaete 1/10,000

Neuve Eglise.
5th. August, 1916.

++++++++++++++++

1. The Left Group consisting of A/172, B/172, C/172 and A/154 18 pdr. Batteries and D/172 Howitzer Battery, assumes the defence of the line from U.1.a.4020 to N.36.c.9080. inclusive. This comprises the following trenches;- The Diagonal - C.2. - C.3. - C.4. - D.1. and D.2.

These trenches are held as follows:-

<u>Right Sector.</u>
The Diagonal }
C.2. } 1 battalion.

<u>Left Sector.</u>
C.3. C.4. }
D.1and D.2. } 1 battalion.

2. The Group Zone on the hostile front line extends from O.31.d.3540 (STEENEBEEK) to N.36.b.0020.

Zones for batteries are as follows:-

<u>Right Sector.</u>

B/172 covers the diagonal - zone on hostile front line O.31.d.3540 to O.31.c.0070

A/172 covers C.2. - zone on hostile front line O.31.c.0070 to U.1.a.1080.

<u>Left Sector.</u>

A/154 covers trenches C.3. and C.4. - zone on hostile front line U.1.a.1080 to N.36.d.5545.

C/172 covers trenches D.1. & D.2. - zone on hostile front line N.36.d.5545 to N.36.b.0020.

D/172 forms the Group Reserve.

3. Battery Commanders will select points in their zones on which their guns will be laid for S.O.S. and gas discharges. These points will be submitted to this Office for consideration and record as soon as possible.
When not firing guns will be kept loaded and laid on these points both day and night.
D/172 will keep 1 section laid on ONTARIO FARM. 1 section on N.36.d.7500.

4. <u>Liaison Officers.</u>

A/172 and B/172 Batteries will in turn provide a liaison officer with the battalion holding the right sector.
A/154 and C/172 Batteries will in turn provide a liaison officer with the battalion holding the left sector.
Liaison Officers will be in duty for 24 hours commencing at 6 p.m.
They will sleep at battalion headquarters and during the day will frequently visit all company headquarters in their sector.

4. contd. They will be provided with sufficient movable twin wire, signallers and signalling equipment, to enable them to direct fire from the front line trench, on any target pointed out to them by the Infantry.

They must be able to communicate with either battery covering the sector so as to engage with the most suitable one.

Liaison Officers will report direct to Group Headquarters when they arrive at battalion headquarters for a tour of duty.

5. Communications.

Batteries will establish direct telephone communication with battalion headquarters of their sectors and company headquarters of the trenches they cover.

The telephonic communication will be supplemented by visual signalling between the infantry and battery O.P's.

6. O.P's will be permanently manned, and an Officer will always be on duty there.

7. Rocket Picquets will be found for each sector nightly. They will consist of an N.C.O. and three Men and will mount at 7 p.m. remaining on duty for 12 hours.

This Picquet will be found in turn by A/172, and B/172 Batteries for the Right Sector and C/172 and A/154 for the Left Sector.

In the Right Sector it will mount near the battery O.P.

Capt. Lockhart will select and report to this Office, a suitable place for the left sector.

The duty of these Picquets is to watch for S.O.S. signals and they must be provided with pointers which will be laid on the points in our trenches where S.O.S. Rockets will be sent up.

D/172 will provide a similar picquet to watch the whole Group Zone. O.C.D/172 is responsible for giving early information of S.O.S. to Group Headquarters.

8. A list of Group Retaliations is attached (Appendix11.)

Local Retaliations must be arranged for by battery and company commanders. When immediate retaliation is required the company commander should call up his "affiliated" battery and give the number or designation of the trench for which retaliation is required. The Battery Commander will then fire on the hostile front line trench opposite. When combined retaliation is required battalion or Brigade Headquarters will communicate with Group Headquarters.

9. Mutual Support.

The following arrangements for mutual support will be carried out:-

A. Support of Centre Group 36th. Division.

B/172 takes up barrage from 0.31.d.6050 to 0.32.c.1000

Support from Centre Group.

1 18 pdr. battery takes up barrage from 0.31.c.8000 to U.1.a.4060.

9 contd. B. Support of Right Group 50th. Division.

C/172 barrages from N.36.b.0020 to N.36.a.7020.

Support from Right Group 50th. Division.

1 18 pdr. battery takes up barrage from N.36.b.0020 to N.36.d.5545.

5.8.16. sd. Adjt.Left Group.

P.S. Copy of Rocket Stations is attached.

Appendix 1.

Retaliations.

ONTARIO.

A/172.	Front Line	U.1.a.8.9½.	to U.1.a.1.8
B/172	Support Line	U.1a.8.9½.	to U.1.a.2.9½
C/172	do.	U.1.a.2.9½	to N.36.d.9.2½
A/154.	do.	U.1.a.½.8	to N.36.d.9.1
D/172	New Trench	0.31.c.7½.1	to 0.31.d.3820.

FACTORY

A/172	Front Line	U.1.a.0.8 to N.36.d.5.6
C/172	CME trenches running back from above front.	
B/172	Support Line	N.36.d.1.1 to N.36.d.7½.7
A/172	FACTORY FARM	
D/172	New Trench	0.31.c.1½.1 to N.36.d.8.7

CROSS ROADS.

C/172	Front Line	N.36.d.2.8 to N.36.a.7.3
A/154	CME trenches running back from above front.	
D/172	Dug-outs at KRUISSTRAAT CABARET and search back to cutting at N.36.b.2½.8	

BACK BLOCKS.

C/172 D/172	ENFER WOOD	
A/154	Battn. H.Q.	0.32.d.6.7.
A/172	Sloping Roof Farm.	
B/172	LX	4 HUNS FARM
	LX	Middle Farm.

(appendex IV)

Operation Orders No.2.[a]

by

Lieut. Col. L.E.S. Ward, D.S.O. R.F.A.

Commanding Left Group.

+++++++++++++++++

Ref. Maps. Wytschaete 1/10,000
Ploegsteert 1/10,000.

Neuve Eglise,
18th August 1916.

1. The Left Group will carry out a bombardment tomorrow of MIDDLE FARM and FOUR HUNS FARM which are reported to be largely used for observation pupposes by the enemy.

Operations will be carried out according to the attached time table. Zero time will be notified.

sd. Adjutant, Left Group.

18-8-16.

10. <u>Mutual Support</u>.

The following arrangements for Mutual Support are in force:-

<u>Support of Centre Group 36th Division.</u>

Left Group gives the following support:-

1 18 pdr Battery (B/172) barrages from U.1.a.6575. to O.31.d.4030.

1 How. on U.1.a.4½.9.) D/172.
1 How. on U.1.a.4½.7½.)

<u>Support from Centre Group</u>.

Centre Group gives the folowing support if the Left Group is attacked:-

1 18 pdr. enfilade trench from U.1.a.7.8¼. upwards.) C/153.
3.18 pdrs. barrage from U.1.a.7.8¼. to U.1.a.6.6¼.)

1 How, on U.1.a.4½.9½)
1 How. on O.31.c.8¼.½.) D/153.

<u>Support of Right Group 19th Division</u>.

Left Group gives the following support to Right Group 19th Division.

C/172. One section 18 pdrs. on trench N.36.b.1.7. to N.30.c.9.5.

D/172. One Howitzer section on cross roads N.36.b.2.8. searching the roads from ~~xxxxx~~ roads from cross roads to N.30.d.10 and N.36.b.0.6.

<u>Support from Right Group 19th Division</u>.

Right Group 19th Division gives the following support if Left Group is attacked:-

1 18 pdr battery will barrage from N.36.d.2078 to N.36.d.5545.

1 section of Howitzers will block N.36.d.7072 and N.36.d.2884 and the junction of communication trenches between hostile front and support lines between these points.

sd. Adjutant, Left Group.

14-8-16.

4. **Liaison Officers.**

A/172 and B/172 batteries in turn provide a liaison officer with the Battalion holding the Right Sector.

A/154 and C/172 in turn provide a liaison officer with the Battalion holding the Left Sector.

Liaison Officers are on duty for 24 hours commencing at 6-0 p.m.

They sleep at Battalion Headquarters and during the day frequently visit all Company Headquarters in their Sector.

The are provided with sufficient movable twin wire, signallers and signalling equipment, to enable them to direct fire front the front line trench, on any target pointed out to them by the Infantry.

They are able to communicate with either battery covering the Sector so as to engage with the most suitable one.

Liaison Officers report by 'phone direct to Group Headquarters when they arrive at Battalion Headquarters for a tour of duty.

5. **Communications.**

Batteries have direct telephone communication with Battalion Headquarters of their sectors and Company Headquarters of the trenches they cover.

This telephonic communication is supplemented by visual signalling between the Infantry and the Battery.

6. **Visual Signalling.**

A/172. From T.6.b.5038 to O.P. (T.18.b.2276) and from there to Battery by lamp.

B/172. Fron C.19. (U.1.a.3015) to O.P. (T.18.b.7072) by lamp from O.P. to Battery by lamp, flags or helios. O.P. Station is 120^{x} from O.P. Runners are used from O.P. Station to O.P.

C/172. N.36.c.9560 to visual Station on KEMMEL HILL (N.26.c.16.) thence by lamp to Battery.

D/172. Owing to the position of the Battery at T.18.d.8.8. on the rear slope of the HILL 63 and the O.P. on the forward slope at T.18.b.8.8. visual signalling for the full distance is impossible, a system of relay stations with runners however is employed.

A/154. Frm C.5. to Farm House beside Battery position at T.3.b.5555.

7. O.Ps are permanently manned and an officer is always on duty there.

8. RocKet Picquets are found for each Sector nightly. They consist of a N.C.O. and three Men and mount at 7 p.m. and remain on duty for 12 hours.

This Picquet is found in turn by A/172, B/172 and D/172 batteries for the Right Sector and C/172 and A/154 for the Left Sector.

In the Right Sector the Picquet mounts at T.18.b.8.7. and in the Left Sector at N.33.b.1035.

The duty of these picquets is to watch for S.O.S. Signals and they are provided with pointers laid on the points in our trenches where S.O.S. Rockets will be sent up.

9. A lsit of Group Retaliations is attached (Appendixl).

Local Retaliation is arranged for by Battery and Company Commanders. When immediate retaliation is required the Company Commander calls up his "affiliated" battery and gives the number or designation of the trench for which retaliation is required. The Battery Commander then fires on the hostile front line trench opposite. When combined retaliation is required Battalion or Brigade Headquarters communicate with Group Headquarters.

SECRET

(appendix III)

Precis of arrangements
LEFT GROUP.
+++++++++++++++++-

1. The Left Group consisting of A/172, B/172, C/172 and A/154 18 pdr. batteries and D/172 Howitzer Battery defends the line from U.1.a.4020 to N.36.c.9080 inclusive. This comprises the following trenches.

The Diagonal - C.2. - C.3. - C.4. - D.1 & D.2.

<u>Right Sector.</u>	<u>Held by</u>	<u>Battn. Hd.Qrs.</u>
The Diagonal C.2.	1 Battalion.	Mc.Brides Mansions. T.6.c.1510.
<u>Left Sector.</u>		
C.3. C.4. D.1. & D.2.	1 Battalion.	St.Quentins Cabaret T.5.d.3.3

2. The Group Zone on the hostile front line extends from O.31.d. 4032 (STEENEBEEK) to N.36.b.0020.

Zones for batteries are as follows:-

<u>Right Sector.</u>

B/172 covers the Diagonal - zone on hostile fron t line O.31.d.4032 to U.1.a.5060.
A/172 covers C.2. - zone on hostile front line U.1.a. 5060 to U.1.a.0080.

<u>Left Sector.</u>

A/154 covers trenches C.3. and C.4. - zone on hostile front line U.1.a.0080 to N.36.d.5545.
C/172 covers trenches D.1. and D.2. - zone on hostile front N.36.d.5545 to N.36.b.0020.
D/172 forms the Group Reserve.

3. <u>Night Lines and S.O.S. Points.</u>

When not firing guns are kept loaded and laid on these points both day and night:-

A/172.
(Night Lines and S.O.S) 1. U.1.a.4565.
2. U.1.a.3065.
3. U.1.a.2070.
4. U.1.a.1075..

B/172. (Night Lines).		S.O.S. Points.
	1. U.1.a.6472.	1. U.1.a.8055.
	2. U.1.a.5565.	2. U.1.a.8065.
	3. U.1.a.7290.	3. U.1.a.7290.
	4. O.31.d.0014.	4. O.31.d.0014.

C/172.
(Night Lines and S.O.S.) 1. N.36.d.5060.
2. N.36.d.3070.
3. N.36.d.1784.
4. N.36.d.1696.

D/172. (Hows.)
(Night Lines and S.O.S) 1. N.36.d.6030.) Where saps leave
2. N.36.d.5840.) front line Trench
3. U.1.a.4592.) Junctions.
4. U.1.a.6078.)

A/154.
(Night Lines and S.O.S. 1. U.1.a.0080.
2. T.6.b.8590.
3.N.36.d.6510.
4.N.36.d.6025.

contd. Rate of fire one round per gun a minute unless otherwise ordered. Duration of retaliation or orders to cease fire will be given from Group Headquarters.

Amendments to
Mutual Support.

The Left Group will give the following support:-

1 18pdr. Battery barrages from U.1.b.6.5½ to 0.31.d.3½.3 B/172.

1 Howitzer on U.1.a.4½.9 D/172
1 do. on U.1.a.4½.7½

The Centre Group gives the following support if the Left Group is attacked:-

1 18 pdr. enfilades from U.i.a.7.8¼)
3 18 pdrs. barrage from U.1.a.7.8¼)
to U.1.a.6.6¼) C/153

1 Howitzer on U.1.a.4½.9½)
1 do. on 0.31.c.8¼.½) D/153

8.8.16. sd. Adjt.Left Group.

(Appendix II)

APPENDIX 2.
to

L.G.Operation Orders No.1.

++++++++++++++++++

Rocket Picquet.

In future a rocket picquet will be found for the right sector by A/172, B/172 and D/172 batteries in turn.

The picquet for the Group Zone found by D/172 will no longer be required.

This picquet will be situated at T.18.b.8.7

Supplement to S.O.S.

In order to enable a Company Commander to obtain artillery support in a tactical situation which does not justify the call for S.O.S. the following procedure will be observed in the left group.

The O.C. Company or Companies concerned will telephone to his supporting battery "Barrage trench......" giving the number of a trench in our line.

On receipt of this message the battery will open fire on the hostile front line opposite the trench named in the message - rate of fire one round per gun per minute.

The receipt of such a message and the action taken by the battery will at once be reported to Group Headquarters.

If the Company Commander considers that the situation requires stronger artillery support he will inform the battery commander who will increase his rate of fire accordingly.

Fire will be continued until the Infantry Commander informs the Battery Commander that the situation no longer requires his support or until an order to cease fire is issued from Group Headquarters.

In the event of other means of communication failing two green VERRY LIGHTS crossed, will be fired from the trench for which support is required.

This is a signal to the Battery covering that particular trench that a barrage is required.

As the situation is obscure the barrage will be a strong one i.e. 3 rounds per gun per minute for ten minutes. after which the rate of fire will be slowed down until the situation becomes clear.

Rocket Picquets must be on the lookout for the Verry Light Sighal and must at once inform the Battery concerned.

The above arrangements must not be confused with the S.O.S. Call.

Combined Retaliations.

The following form of message will be sent from Group Headquarters when a combined retaliation is to be carried out:-

"Retaliate FACTORY 2 p.m."

On receipt of such a message batteries concerned will open fire on the tasks for "FACTORY" retaliation given in Appendix 1. Operation Order No.1. d/-5.8.16.

Instructions regarding War Diaries and Intelligence Summaries are contained in F. S. Regs., Part II. and the Staff Manual respectively. Title Pages will be prepared in manuscript.

WAR DIARY
or
~~INTELLIGENCE~~ SUMMARY
(Erase heading not required.)

172nd Bde R.F.A.

Vol 10

Army Form C. 2118.

Place	Date	Hour	Summary of Events and Information	Remarks and references to Appendices
In the Field	1.9.16		A quiet day – visited O.Ps of A, B and D Batteries. Weather overcast & warm.	THM
	2.9.16		A very quiet night. Visited all trenches (first line) and tested all Artillery communications also visited both battalion H.Q. and saw all Company Commanders. Inspected C/172 Wagon line. Operations for night 2/3 cancelled owing to unfavourable wind. Weather fine – cloudy – hot	THM
	3.9.16		Gas Alert given about 9 pm. At 10.20 pm gas alarm given from Right Group did not however fire as information was too vague. Conference of Brigade Commanders on re-organization. Weather overcast – cloudy & hot	THM
	4.9.16		Some artillery fire during the night. Re-organization scheme commenced. New scheme of retaliations compiled. (appendix I) Visited battery positions C/172 & A.154. Weather overcast – heavy showers – warm.	THM app: I
	5.9.16		Discharge of gas again cancelled during the night. Inspected battery positions C/172 & B/172. Left Group Operation Order No. 1. issued. (appendix 2) Weather – wet – temperature warm.	THM app: II
	6.9.16		About 10 pm night 5/6th information received that Enemy was carrying out relief – all batteries opened fire at a slow rate with occasional bursts. Instructions received to keep hostile communications under fire as XXIIIrd Corps (German) was under relief. Table of Group concentrations issued. (appendix III) ~~[illegible] left Centre front issued~~ Left Centre front O.O. No. 1. carried out at 2 pm. Weather fine & warm – very good	THM app: III
	7.9.16		Concentration No. 4 issued (appendix IV) Some artillery activity during night 6/7th according to programme. Group concentrations Nos. 1 & 3 carried out. Visited wagon lines of A, B & D Batteries. Weather fine & warm	THM app IV

2449 Wt. W14957/M90 750,000 1/16 J.B.C. & A. Forms/C.2118/12.

(app. IV)

Appendix 1. to this Office No.353/172.

dated 6.9.1916.

+++++++++++++++++++++++

Concentration 4. L'ENFER.

B/172. Enfilades tracks from O.26.a.3112 to O.26.c.0459.

A/172. Enfilades valley O.25.d.9248 to O.25.d. 8024.

A/154. Ground in rear of knoll 62 from O.26.c. 0075 to O.25.b.9000.

C/172. Enfilades valley from O.25.b.5818 to O.25.d.2871.

D/172. Buildings at O.25.d.8279.

[signature]

2/Lt. R.F.A.

7.9.1916. Adjt.172nd. Bde. R.F.A.

(appendix I)

Revised List of Retaliations.

The following organized retaliations will be taken into use in the Group from 5th. September, in place of "ONTARIO", "FACTORY" etc.,

Retaliation A.

B/172.	Hostile front and support lines.	U.1.a.6273 to O.31.c.9015.	Enfilade
A/172	Hostile reserve line.	O.31.c.7505 to O.31.c.4506.	Sweep.
A/154.	Hostile reserve line	O.31.c.4506 to O.31.c.1810.	Sweep
D/172	Hostile support line.	U.1.a.7095 to U.1.a.4393. and U.1.a.2986 to O.31.c.1007.	

Retaliation B.

B/172.	Hostile reserve line.	O.31.c.0037 to N.36.d.9256.
A/172	do.	N.36.d.9256 to N.36.d.8274.
A/154.	Hostile support line.	N.36.d.9225 to N.36.d.7838.
C/172.	do.	N.36.d.7838 to N.36.d.7260.
D/172.	Blocks hostile trenches at following points:-	

O.31.c.0037 }
N.36.d.8274. } hostile reserve line.

N.36.d.9225 }
N.36.d.7260. } hostile support line.

Retaliation C.

A/172.	Hostile reserve line.	N.36.d.8380 to N.36.b.~~[illegible]~~.7000
A/154.	do.	N.36.b.~~[illegible]~~ 7000 to N.36.b.5816.
C/172.	do.	N.36.b.5816 to N.36.b.4227.
D/172.	Blocks following points:-	

O.31.c.0344.
~~N.36.d~~.0344 }
N.36.d.9668 } Communication trenches.

N.36.d.8380 }
N.36.b.4227. } Hostile reserve line.

Retaliation D.

(Four Huns Farm)

B/172.	Hostile trench	O.32.a.6685 to O.26.c.6000
A/172.	Hedge S.of Farm.	O.32.a.5583 to O.32.a.9890.
A/154.	Hedge N.of Farm.	O.26.c.4223 to O.26.c.8532.
C/172.	Hostile trench	O.26.c.6000 to O.26.c.5822.
D/172.	Farm buildings.	

When any of these retaliations are to be used batteries concerned will be notified by telephone message worded "Retaliation B" AAA followed by time for duration of operation and number of rounds per gun.

W A Edmenson
2/Lt. R.F.A.
Adjt.172nd. Bde. R.F.A.

4.9.1916.

Copies

1. File.
2. War Diary.
3. O.C.A/172.
4. O.C.B/172.
5. O.C.C/172.
6. O.C.D/172.
7. O.C.A/154.
8. B.M.36th. Div. Arty.

(appendix 2)

OPERATION ORDERS NO. 1.

by

Lieut. Col. L.E.S. Ward, D.S.O., R.F.A.

Commanding Left Centre Group.

Ref. Map. MESSINES Sheet 8, 1/10,000.

Neuve Eglise,
5th September 1916.

1. A bombardment for the destruction of a portion of the enemy's front line will be carried out on September 6th 1916, commencing at 4 p.m.

2. Battery tasks are shown on attached table.

The following units are taking part in addition to the whole Left Centre Group:-

1½ Batteries of 6" Howitzers.
D/173 Battery.
D/86th. Battery.
Left Group 18 pdr. Batteries.
2" Trench Mortars.

3. The bombardment will commence with one salvo from each battery and will afterwards continue at a steady rate of fire till allotted ammunition is expended. After the salvos the rate of fire will be section fire 30 seconds making the period of bombardment 50 minutes.

4. Watches will be synchronized by telephone at 12 noon + 2 pm and 3 p.m. 6th. instant.

5. The Group Commander will be at the O.P. D/172 during the operation.

Acknowledge.

W.A. Edmenson
2/Lt. R.F.A.
Adjt.172nd. Bde. R.F.A

5.9.1916.

Table of Tasks for Operation Order No.1.
::

Battery.	Time.	Task.	Ammn.	Remarks.
B/172.	4 p.m.	Hostile front line from N.36.d.7005 to N.36.d.6810. Communication trench commencing at N.36.d. 7007 to N.36.d.9812.	150 AX 50 A	Communication trenches to be sprayed with shrapnel
A/172.	do.	Hostile front line from N.36.d.6810 to N.36.d.6719. Hostile communication trench commencing at N.36.d.6719 to N.36.d. 9234.	do.	do.
A/154.	do.	Hostile front line from N.36.d.6719 to N.36.d. 6222. Communication trenches commencing at N.36.d. 9234 and N.36.d.9812.	do.	do.
C/172	do.	Hostile front line N.36.d.6222 to N.36.d. 6325. Communication trench commencing at N.36.d. 6325 to N.36.d.9038.	do.	do.
D/172.	do.	N.36.d.6615 - N.36.d. 6030 and junction of communication trench and support trench at N.36.d.8235.	200.	One gun on each junction

353/172.

(appendix III

From:- Adjutant 172nd. Brigade. R.F.A.

To:- O.C.

Ref. Map. Messines Sheet 8.
1/10,000

1. From information received it is supposed that the German XXIII Reserve Corps will be relieved during the next few days.

2. 18 pdr. Batteries will bombard the enemy's front support and communication trenches and any routes, possible points of assembly, and lines of approach in their Zones.

3. For the above purposes batteries will take as their zone boundaries imaginary lines drawn N.E. from the points given as boundaries on the hostile front line vide Precis of Operation Orders dated 14.8.1916.

4. The following group concentrations will come into force:-

Concentration 1. Messines - St. Eloi Road.

D/172. commencing at O.32.b.1053 sweeps up Messines St. Eloi Road for 200 yards.
B/172. commencing at O.32.b.0090 sweeps as above.
A/172. commencing at O.26.c.9020 sweeps as above.
A/154. commencing at O.26.c.8050 sweeps as above.
C/172. commencing at O.26.c.7080 sweeps as above.

Concentration 2. Cross Roads in O.31.a.

B/172. searches road N.36.d.8376 to Cross Roads O.31.a.0240.
A/172. searches road from O.31.a.0240 to O.25.c.3000
A/154. searches road from O.31.a.0240 to O.31.a.4023.
C/172. searches road from N.36.b.5061 to O.31.a.0240.
D/172. searches cuttings running N. and S.E. from Cross Roads at O.31.a.0240.

Concentration 3. Road in O.31.a.b & d.

Commencing with C/172 at O.31.a.5017 batteries in order from the left sweep 200 yards of road.

The application of these concentrations will be notified be telephone in the following form "Concentration two AAA time 6.30 p.m. AAA three rounds gun fire five seconds (or salvos)"

5. The above orders will hold good during the next three or four days.

2/Lt. R.F.A.
Adjt.172nd. Bde. R.F.A.

6.9.1916.

To OC A B C D A/154
Bn 36 DA

Army Form C. 2118.

WAR DIARY
or
~~INTELLIGENCE~~ SUMMARY
(Erase heading not required.)

Instructions regarding War Diaries and Intelligence Summaries are contained in F. S. Regs., Part II. and the Staff Manual respectively. Title Pages will be prepared in manuscript.

Place	Date	Hour	Summary of Events and Information	Remarks and references to Appendices
In the Field	8.9.16		front Concentrations 1 & 2 & 4 carried out during the night. Visited gun positions of all batteries in the front during the day. Arrangements made to cover front with 3 batteries instead of four. Weather fine & warm.	T.H.M
			appendix to orders of arrangement left Centre front issued (appendix V)	App: V
	9.9.16		Hostile Artillery active during night especially about Neuve Eglise. Conference at front H.Q. 153rd Bde. All Brigade Commanders & O.C. D.A.C. present. Centre front O.O. No 1 issued (appendix VI) Weather fine & warm.	T.H.M App VI
	10.9.16		A quiet night. Visited new position of C/172 battery and B/172. also visited wagon lines B & C Batteries. Weather overcast & warm.	T.H.M
	11.9.16		Hostile Aeroplanes dropped bombs in vicinity – no casualties to Brigade. Re-organization commenced. Weather fine & warm.	T.H.M
	12.9.16		A very quiet night. Re-organization continued. Visited wagon lines of B/172 battery and inspected work on horse standings. Weather fine & warm.	T.H.M
	13.9.16		Night again very quiet. Change over of right & centre groups carried out. Right front O.O. No. 1 issued. (appendix VII) Weather wet with heavy showers. appendix 1 to O.O. (Right front) No 1 issued (appendix VIII) Retaliations in three areas Left, Centre & Right issued (appendix IX)	T.H.M App. VII App VIII App IX
	14.9.16		Some artillery fire during the night. Made complete tour of trenches in new zone visiting all Company & Battalion Headquarters & tested all communications which were found to be unsatisfactory. Brigade communications – officer spent remainder of day in putting them in order & reported them as satisfactory at 9 pm. (appendix 2 to Right front O.O. issued) (appendix X)	T.H.M App. X

2449 Wt. W14957/M90 750,000 1/16 J.B.C. & A. Forms/C.2118/12.

APPENDIX TO PRECIS OF ARRANGEMENTS. *appendix V*

LEFT CENTRE GROUP.

Ref. Map. MESSINES Sheet 8. 1/10,000 Neuve Eglise.
8th. September, 1916

1. Change of Zones. The following changes in battery zones will come into force at 9 a.m. 9th. September.

Right Sector.

B/172 covers the diagonal and C.2. - zone on hostile front O.31.d.4032 to U.1.a.1077.

Left Sector.

A/172 covers trenches C.3. and C.4. - zone on hostile front line U.1.a.1077 to N.36.d.6225.

A/154. covers trenches D.1 and D.2. - zone on hostile front line N.36.d.6225 to N.36.d.1495.

For the purpose of night lines and S.O.S. D/172 will transfer one section from sap heads at N.36.d.5060 and N.36.d.3070 and take up points on the section U.1.a.2570 to U.1.a.1077. O.C.B/172 will take this into consideration in arranging his night and S.O.S. lines.

Battery Commanders will select points for night lines and S.O.S. in accordance with the above changes in zones and report their arrangements to Group Headquarters before 6 p.m. 9th. September.

2. Liaison Officers. Liaison Officers will be found by A/154 and A/172 batteries for the left sector and B/172 and D/172 batteries for the right sector.

There is no change in the duties and duration of tour for liaison Officers.

3. Communications. The Brigade Orderly Officer in conjunction with Battery Commanders will make all necessary arrangements for communications to suit the new distribution. Visual signalling will be established under Battery Commander's arrangements, arrangements to be reported to Group Headquarters before 7 p.m. 9th. September.

4. Rocket Picquets. Rocket Picquets will be found for the Right Sector by B/172 and D/172 batteries and for the left sector by A/172 and A/154, batteries.

2/Lt. R.F.A.
Adjt.172nd. Bde. R.F.A.

8.9.1916.

Copies to
1. File.
2. Diary.
3. O.C.A/172.
4. O.C.B/172.
5. O.C.C/172.
6. O.C.D/172.
7. O.C.A/154.
8. B.M.36th. Div. Arty.
9. B.M.107th. Inf. Bde.

(Appendix VI)

Operation Order No.1.

CENTRE GROUP.

By

Lieut. Col. L.E.S.Ward, D.S.O., R.F.A.

::::::::::::::::::::

Ref. Map. MESSINES Sheet 8. 1/10,000 Neuve Eglise,
9th. September, 1916.

1. In the event of a discharge of gas taking place on the Group Front batteries will co-operate by a bombardment of the hostile front and support lines. Battery Zones for this operation are given in attached table.

2. A raid on hostile trenches will take place after the emission of gas.

This raid will be carried out by a detail from 107th Infantry Brigade.

The point of entry is at N.36.d.2078.

3. No artillery preparation for the raid is to be carried out.

4. During the raid batteries as detailed below will "stand by" to assist if necessary.

Battery Tasks.

B/172 will barrage hostile front line from N.36.d.3565 to N.36.d.5350.
A/154 will barrage hostile front line from N.36.d.1593 to N.36.b.0306.
A/172 will barrage hostile reserve line from N.36.b.6800 to N.36.d.8376.

Rates of fire for 18 pdrs. 1round per gun for 30 minutes, followed by 1 round per gun for 10 minutes.

D/172 will block the following points:-

N.36.b.2200.
N.36.d.3590.
N.36.d.4881.

Rates of fire 1 round per gun for 30 minutes.

5. Time of discharge of gas 1-30 a.m.
Time artillery open fire 1-34 a.m.
do do cease fire 2-4 a.m.

Time of commencement of raid 2-30 a.m. Guns will be laid for the operation by this hour.

6. The signal for ~~the~~ artillery action to assist the raiding party if necessary will be three Verry Lights fired simultaneously as "Prince of Wales Feathers", see diagram.

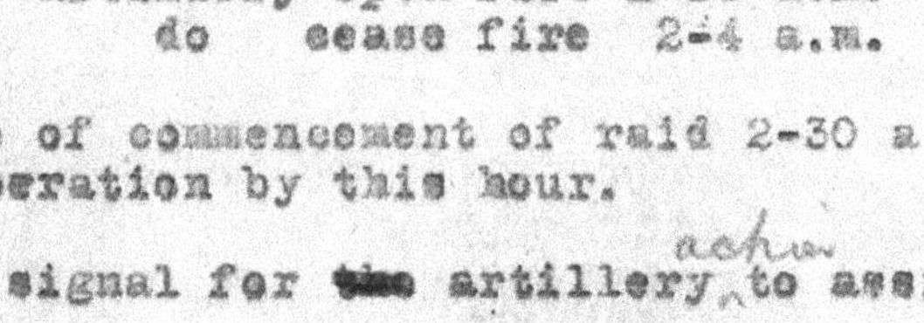

7. Batteries detailed for this operation will make arrangements for observation posts specially detailed to look out for this signal and communicate its appearance at once to their batteries.

The signal will be sent up from the near vicinity of N.36.d.2078 and pointers should be laid on this point.

O.C.D/172 is responsible for reporting the signal to Group H.Q. The word "Feathers" will be telephoned.

If the signal for assistance does not appear, ordinary night lines will be resumed 1½ hours after the time arranged for the raid to begin.

If the signal is given and no further information comes to hand night lines will be resumed 30 minutes after batteries cease fire.

8. If the discharge of gas is not to take place batteries will be informed by telephone, the word "NO" being sent. On receipt of this message ordinary night duties will be resumed.

9. Left Group Operation Orders Nos. 4 & 5 are cancelled.

10. Acknowledge.

W.A. Edmenson.
2/Lt. R.F.A.
9.9.1916. Adjt.172nd. Brigade. R.F.A

Copies to

1. File.
2. Diary.
3. O.C.A/172.
4. O.C.B/172.
5. O.C.C/172.
6. O.C.D/172.
7. O.C.A/154.
8. B.M.36th. Div. Arty.
9. B.M.107th. Inf. Bde.

Battery.	Hour.	Task.	Rate of fire.	Remarks.
B/172.	1.34 a.m. to 2.4. a.m.	O.31.c.7500 to U.1.a.0079	1.34 a.m. to 1.40 a.m. Section fire 10 secs. 1.40 a.m. to 2.2.a.m.Section fire15 secs. 2.2 a.m. to 2.4 a.m. Section fire 5 secs.	Search and sweep.
A/172.	do.	U.1.a.0079 to N.36.d.6030.	do	
A/154.	do.	N.36.d.6030 to N.36.d.1595.	do.	
D/172.	do.	One section ONTARIO FARM from U.1.a.6078 to point in hostile support line U.1.a.1795 One section from FACTORY FARM & hostile support line from N.36.d.9224 to N.36.d.7066.	Section fire 20 secs.	Sweep

Appendix VII

Operation Order No.1.

RIGHT GROUP

by

Lieut. Col. L.E.S. Ward D.S.O. R.F.A.

::::::::::::::::::::::

Ref Map. Ploegsteert Edition 3.D. 1/10000

Neuve Eglise,
11th September 1916.

1. Composition. The Group consists of 2 18-pdr batteries and one 4.5" Howitzer battery, viz:-

A/172.	18-pdr. Battery.	6 guns.
B/172.	do.	6 guns.
D/172.	4.5" Howitzer.	4 guns.

2. Distribution. The Group covers trenches 134 to 142 inclusive.

Right Sector.

B/172 covers tranches 134, 135, 136 and 137- zone on hostile front line U.8.b.0020 to U.2.c.6092 (Road inclusive).

The sector is held by one battalion.

Battalion Headquarters at STINKING FARM U.7.a.5070.

Company Headquarters at (C21.) (~~x.x.x.xxxx~~ U1a 8060)-(C.25) (U.8.a.2595).

Left Sector.

A/172 covers trenches 138, 139, 140, 141, 142, zone on hostile front line U.~~1~~2.c.6092 (Road exclusive) to O.31.d.4034.

The sector is held by one battalion.

Battalion Headquarters at T.12.a.7080. FISHERS PLACE.

Campany Headquarters at C.45 (U.1.b.2000)-(C.38) BOYLES FARM (U.1.a.4000)-(C.13) (U.1.d.9550).

Battery Commanders will select points for Night Lines, S.O.S. and Gas Alarm and report them to Group Headquarters as soon as possible.

D/172 forms the Group Reserve and covers the whole Group Zone.

Battery Commander will lay guns for night lines - S.O.S. and Gas Alarm on the following points:-

O.31.d.6144.
U.2.a.1750.
U.2.d.1252.
U.8.a.9253.

3.
Communications. Each Battery will be connected by telephone to the H.Q. of the Battalion it covers and to company headquarters in the trenches.

Battery Commanders will arrange for visual signalling from the front line to O.P's and between O.P's and batteries.

4.
Liaison Officers. B/172 Battery will find a Liaison Officer with the Right Sector and A/172 will find a Liaison Officer with the Left Sector.

Liaison Officers will report to battalion headquarters at 9 p.m. nightly and their tour of duty will end at one hour after "Stand to".

Liaison Officers will be accompanied by a telephonist and any necessary equipment.

Liaison Officers will render a short telephonic report to Group Headquarters at the expiration of their tour of duty.

Battery Commanders will arrange for Officers to make frequent visits to the Company Headquarters of the Units they cover.

5.
Rocket Picquet. All batteries in turn will find a rocket picquet of 1 N.C.O. and 3 men.

The Picquet will mount at the "CELLARS".

The duty of this picquet is to watch for all Rocket Signals emanating from our own lines and report immediately to Group Headquarters and Batteries, through the telephone exchange at the "CELLARS". The Battery finding the rocket picquet will also find two telephonists at the "CELLARS" Exchange.

Pointers will be laid on the Rocket Stands as detailed below, to ensure the identification of the point from which ~~it~~ a signal is sent up.

Rocket Stands are situated at the following points:-

<u>Right Section.</u> (Composite Battalion)

One stand extreme left of trench 134.
One stand between bays 9 and 10 Trench 136.
One stand at STINKING FARM.

<u>Centre Section.</u>

One stand in Trench 140.
One stand Battalion H.Q. FISHERS VILLAS
(T.12.a.7.7)

<u>Left Section.</u>

One stand in trench 142 behind bay 6.
One stand Battalion H.Q. MC.BRIDES MANSIONS.

Rocket Picquets mount at 6.30 p.m. and come off duty at 6.30a.m.

Telephonists at the CELLARS will be on duty from 6.30 p.m. to 6.30 p.m.

6.
<u>Retaliation.</u> In the event of a hostile barrage being put down on any trench or trenches, the O.C. Company, or Companies, concerned will immediately telephone to his supporting Artillery "BARRAGE TRENCH ------------

On this message the Battery Commander concerned will open section fire 30 seconds, and at once inform Group H.Q. of his action. He will only stop on an order to that effect being sent in from this Office.

The expression "BARRAGE TRENCH --------- means fire is to be brought on the enemy trench opposite the one of ours named.

In the event of the enemy barrage lifting, the same Company Commander will send up two White Very Lights crossed

as a signal to the Artillery that an intense barrage is required where the signal is displayed. Similar arrangements will be made as before with the exception that the rate of fire will be quickened to section fire 10 seconds.

In the event of the telephone line being cut in the first instance the Very Light Signal mentioned above will be used instead.

These arrangements have nothing whatever to do with the "S.O.S. Signal".

Special instructions on each occasion will be issued to the Howitzer Battery as to their fire.

7. (1) The S.O.S. call will be a "PRIORITY" Call, and will be
S.O.S. preceded by the "STOP" Signal and followed by the number of the trench, trenches or sector being attacked, e.g.,

S.O.S. 134.

S.O.S. 137 - 139.

or S.O.S. Right Sector, or Left Sector.

This signal will be passed to all stations on his lines by the Artillery Telephonist receiving it.

(2) The battery or batteries responsible for the portion attacked will immediately fire three rounds gun fire, sweeping the necessary amount, and then battery fire 10 secs. or section fire 20 seconds, still sweeping to cover their own front, the rate of fire being increased or decreased as the situation demands.

The Battery on each flank of the above battery or batteries will turn on to the portion of the enemy trenches in front of the point attacked, and open with a similar rate of fire

(3) The remaining batteries of the Division will each switch towards the point attacked, on to the barrage lines of the battery next to them, and open fire at Section Fire 30 secs.

The flank batteries of the Divisions on the right and left will conform. The rate of fire being increased or decreased as the situation demands.

By this means the barrage in front of the trench or trenches being attacked will be increased by the fire of two batteries while the rest of the front will be still covered by the original number of batteries.

Batteries will switch a section at a time in order that there may be no pause in firing.

(4) The fire will be kept up on these barrage lines until Group Commanders receive information as to the situation, when they can, of course, be altered by them to suit requirements.

(5) The S.O.S. Rocket Signal in use by the 2nd. Army is used asx a supplementary signal only. The colour of the

rocket is altered from time to time by order of the 2nd. Army. At the present time it is ~~red~~. Green.

This rocket will only be used as a signal that the enemy is issuing from his trenches on our front to attack.

It is not used to denote gas attacks, explosion of mines etc., nor merely because rockets have been fired by Brigades on our flanks.

(6) The signal will be one rocket, which will be repeated until the artillery open fire.

(7) The signal will be supplemented by telephone messages explaining the situation.

(8) If the Rocket Signal is seen and no "S.O.S" call has been received on the telephone, all batteries will immediately fire three rounds gun fire on their Night Barrage Lines, and then will switch by Sections towards that portion of the enemy trenches in front of which the rocket has gone up, and continue firing as laid down in paras. 2 & 3.

8 Gas. On the GAS ALARM sounding, batteries will immediately open a slow rate of fire, 1 round per battery per minute, with H.E. on their barrage lines on the enemy's front line parapet. This will be kept up until the "S.O.S" Signal is sent, when batteries will act as laid down in "Instructions for S.O.S" When it is ascertained from which part of the German trenches the gas is coming batteries responsible for that portion of the line will open a quicker rate of fire with a view to destroying the enemy's parapet and gas cylinders.

9
Mutual Support.

1. If the Right Group is attacked:-

a. The Left Group 19th. Division willz give the following support:-

2 sections will barrage from U.8.b.0040 to U.8.b.0065.
1 section Hows: will fire as follows:-
1 gun on U.8.b.28
1 gun on U.2.d.43

b. Support given to Left Group 19th. Division.

B/172. 2 sections from U.8.b.12 to U.8.a.9½.4
2 do do U.8.d.7½.9 to U.8.b.60

D/172. 1 How. will fire on U.9.c.09
1 How. will fire on U.8.b.44

2. a. The Centre Group gives the following support if the Right Group is attacked:-

2 sections 18 pdr. battery enfilades and barrages from U.1.a.6575 to O.31.d.4032.
1 How. will fire on U.1.a.4½.9
1 How. do. do. U.1.a.4½.7½.

b. Right Group gives the following support if the Centre Group is attacked:-

A/172. 2 sections enfilade and barrage from U.1.a. 6575 to O.31.d.4032.

D/172. 1 How. on U.1.a.4½.9
1 How. on O.31.c.8¼.¼

10
Selected Squares.

U.2. for A/172.
U.3. for B/172.

11.
General.

On the order "Test all" 1 round per gun is fired by all batteries in the Group on their night lines.

Appendix 1 gives detail of retaliation: (will be forwarded tomorrow).

12.9.1916.

2/Lt. R.F.A.
Adjt.172nd. Bde. R.F.A

Copies to

1. File.
2. Diary.
3. O.C. A/172.
4. O.C.B/172.
5. O.C.D/172.
6. B.M.36th. D.A.
7. B.M.108th. Inf. Bde.

Appendix VIII

Appendix 1 to

Operation Order (Right Group) No.1.

:::::::::::::::::::

Please read for selected squares in para.10

Operation Orders No.1.

A/172. U.8. B/172. U.28 3.

W A Edmenson
2/Lt. R.F.A.
Adjt. 172nd. Bde.R.F.A.

13.9.1916.

Copies.

1. File.
2. Diary.
3. O.C.A/172.
4. O.C.B/172.
5. O.C.D/172.
6. B.M.36th. D.A.
7. B.M.108th. Inf. Bde.

App: IX

Retaliation in three Areas, Left, Centre and Right.

::

Code Letter "A"

<u>Left Area</u> A/172 Enemy Communication Trenches and support line in U.2.a.

B/172 Area U.2.c.9.8 and the GULLY

D/172 (How) BON FERMIER CABARET & ST.HOSPICE.

Code Letter "B"

<u>Centre Area</u> A/172 Communication Trenches and support lines U.2.c.N.E. and U.2.d.North.

B/172 Top of LOOP.

D/172 Top end of LOOP and WORKS

Code Letter "C"

<u>Right Area</u> A/172 Loop about U.2.d.Central GULLY and Communication trench. U.8.d.1.3 - 4.7.

B/172 Dug-out line behind PETITE DOUVE, Lower end of LOOP Communication Trench U,8.b.

D/172 Lower end of LOOP.

<u>Reference "A" "B" & "C"</u>

O.C's will select objectives in zone named which are best calculated to suffer damage from the direction of their fire and can be clearly observed. Orders etc., for quickly turning on will be known to all concerned.

<u>ORDERS WILL BE GIVEN THUS</u> -

Retaliation "A" 10.0 a.m. etc.

If no number of rounds or duration is added, 18 pdrs will fire 30 rounds each and 4.5" How: 15 rounds in 5 minutes from the time named, only general observation of effect being possible Usually the time and number of rounds to be fired would be added to the message unless extreme rapidity is necessary. If fire was required for special slow retaliation the Batteries would fire in succession at a named map point or line, thus -

Example only "Slow retaliation (U.2.c.1.1 - U.2.c.5.2)
18 pdrs; 30 rds 4.5" How: 30 rds. 15 minutes each from 11 a.m.

The 18 pdrs fire in succession B/172 and A/172 for 15 minutes each and D/172 for the whole period - 30 minutes spreading rounds allotted to it over the period, fire would be observed and corrected in all cases.

Retaliation for minenwerfers trench mortars will be given as quickly as possible by covering batteries and D/172 How: the latter should get the information passed on from O.P. Signal Exchange direct as regards the right sector.

In left sector D/172 should, when asked to retaliate for TMs at once inform H.Q. or the "CELLARS" (O.P.) to pass the word to the How: Battery.

A very rough message would do such as "Minnie Petite Douve" or "Minnies U.2.c.2.8" etc.,

Machine Guns are numbered and a list will be issued shortly.

Positions of Trench Mortars which have been located in our areas are as follows:-

1. U.9.c.2.8
2. U.2.d.1½.5
3. U.2.d.9.9
4. U.2.d.3½.8
5. U.3.c.7.8
6. The LOOP
7. U.9.b.½.7
8. U.8.b1½.2.
9. U.8.b.3.3
10. U.2.a.8.½
11. U.3.a.7.0

Those recently in use are (2) (1) (8) (9)

If Group Retaliation on T.M's becomes necessary:-

"Minnies Left" include (1) (2) (10)
"Minnies Centre" " (3) to (6) (11)
"Minnies Right" " PETITE DOUVE & (7) to (9)
followed by message "Group concentrate"

Any fresh positions will be added to these lists as located.

If concentration on any single T.M. is required the map location will be given.

System of fire etc., as for ordinary retaliations.

W.A. Edmenson.
2/Lt. R.F.A.
Adjt.172nd. Bde.R.F.A.

14.9.1916.

App. X

Appendix 2 to Operation Order No.1.

RIGHT GROUP.

:::::::::::::::::::::::::::::::::::

Reference para. 2 (Distribution) Right Sector please read Right Sub-Sector, and also Left Sub-Sector.

Reference para.9. (Mutual Support) Support given to Left Group 19th. Division, for B/172 2 Sections please read B/172 1 section in each case.

W.A. Edmenson.
2/Lt. R.F.A.
Adjt.172nd. Brigade. R.F.A

14.9.1916.

Copies to

1. File.
2. Diary.
3. O.C.A/172.
4. O.C.B/172.
5. O.C.D/172.
6. B.M.36th. D.A.
7. B.M.108th. Inf. Bde.

Army Form C. 2118.

WAR DIARY
or
~~INTELLIGENCE SUMMARY~~
(Erase heading not required.)

Instructions regarding War Diaries and Intelligence Summaries are contained in F. S. Regs., Part II. and the Staff Manual respectively. Title Pages will be prepared in manuscript.

Place	Date	Hour	Summary of Events and Information	Remarks and references to Appendices
In the Field	15.9.16		Normal activity during the night. Visited all O.P. & went over points in zone. Fixed S.O.S. lines A Battery. Weather fine but colder.	Thm
	16.9.16		Visited battery positions A & B & wagon lines A.B. & D. Weather warm & bright	Thm
	17.9.16		Conference at 153rd Bde H.Q. Visited O.P. of B Battery & inspected three proposed O.Ps for A & B batteries. Weather fine & warm. (appen 36 O.O. No.1 issued) (append: X A)	Thm app: XA
	18.9.16		Inspected all trench mortar positions in front Zone accompanied by C.R.E who advised on constructive details. Weather - heavy rain until 4 pm.	Thm
	19.9.16		Visited wagon lines of all batteries. Front very quiet. Weather fine till about 12.30 pm after which heavy showers at intervals.	Thm
	20.9.16		Some artillery fire during the night. Visited proposed O.Ps with battery commanders, also saw B/172 fire on night lines. Work on horse lines progressing. Weather overcast during morning - heavy rain during the afternoon - cold.	Thm
	21.9.16		Night normal. Inspected wagon line of D Battery. Attended Conference on subject of raids to be made by 108th Inf. Bde. Weather - overcast but no rain - wind varied from N to NE "dangerous". O.O. No.3 issued (appendix X B.)	Thm app: XB
	22.9.16		About 12.30 pm gas alarm given but proved false. Col. Ward left at 6.0 pm for R.A. H.Q. to take temporary command of the Divisional Artillery whilst General Brock is away on leave. Capt. J.A. Sebag-Montefiore in temporary command of the Bde, Major Bolitho being away on leave. Amendment to O.O. No.1 issued (appendix XC)	Thm app XC
	23.9.16		Enemy's attitude still very passive. Weather - warm sunshine - wind dangerous.	

2449 Wt. W14957/M90 750,000 1/16 J.B.C. & A. Forms/C.2118/12.

App. X A

Appendix 3 to Operation Order No.1.

RIGHT GROUP

By

Lieut. Col. L.E.S. Ward, D.S.O., R.F.A. 17.9.1916.

::::::::::::::::::::::

For Mutual Support 19th. Division please insert the following and cancel previous instructions:-

a. Support from 19th. Division.

B/86

Right Section enfilade from U.8.b.4½.4½ to U.9.a.0.7
Centre Section do. do. U.9.b.2.8 to U.2.d.5.3
Left Section do. do. U.8.a.9.7 to U.2.d.1½.0

D/86 will shell, with one gun, F.L.T. U.8.a.9½.2 to U.8.b.0.5 (in enfilade)
1 gun from U.8.a.8½.4½ to U.8.a.9½.7 (in enfilade)
1 gun in Trench Junction U.8.b. 4½.4½.
1 gun do. do. U.8.b.2.7.

Code Word "Co-operate with Left"

Rate of Fire B/86 12 rounds per Battery per minute

D/86 Gun fire 30 seconds.

b. Support given to 19th. Division if attacked:-

B/172	2	18 pdrs.	Trench U.8.b.4.4 to U.8.b.8.7
	4	18 pdrs.	Trench U.8.b.4.4 to U.8.b.8.4
D/172	1	4.5" How:	LA PETITE DOUVE FARM
	1	4.5" How:	Trench Junction U.8.b.4.4

Call for co-operation will be "Co-Operate 19th. Division"

W.A. Edmenson.
2/Lt. R.F.A.
Adjt.172nd. Bde.R.F.A

17.9.1916.

Copies to

1. File,
2. Diary.
3. O.C.A/172.
4. O.C.B/172.
5. O.C.D/172.
6. B.M.36th. Div. Arty.
7. B.M.108th. Inf. Bde.

(app: XB) 11

O P E R A T I O N   O R D E R   NO. 3.

by

Lieut. Col., L.M.S. Ward D.S.O. R.F.A.

Commanding Right Group.   21-9-16.

Ref. Map. PLOEGSTEERT 1/10,000.

1. A combined bombardment of the hostile defence about La PETITE DOUVE will be carried out on Friday September 22nd 1916.

2. The following units will take part:-

A/172	)	
B/172	)	18-pdr batteries.
D/172		4.5" How. Battery.
X/36		2" Trench Mortar Battery (2guns).
V/36		1 heavy Trench Mortar.
108th.		Stokes Mortar Battery (4 guns).

Tasks as per attached schedule.

3. The operation will commence at 3 p.m.

Registration will be carried out during the morning.

"B" Battery 172, will cover the trench mortars while registering. Times to be arranged by O.C. "B" Battery and O.C. 36th Divisional Trench Mortars.

2nd Lieut. R.F.A.,
f/Actg.Adjt. 172nd Bde. R.F.A.

B A T T E R Y   T A S K S.

Batty.	Hour.	Task.	Ammunition.	Remarks.
B/172. 18 pr.	3-0 p.m. to 3-30 p.m.	Hostile support Line U.8.b.4923 to U.2.d.3800.	5 rounds per gun.	Sweep.
A/172.	3-55 p.m. to 4-0 p.m.	as above.	do.	do.
D/172.	3 p.m. to 4 p.m.	The following points U.8.b.4520. U.8.b.4650. U.8.b.4040. U.8.b.3964. U.8.b.2384.	do.	
Z/36 T.M.	do.	Hostile front line about LA PETITE DOUVE from U.8.b.0122 to U.8.a.8758.	4 rounds per gun.	Search & Sweep.
108th Stokes Mortars.	do.	Hostile front line from U.8.a. 8758 to U.2.d.1303.	100 rds per gun.	Bursts of fire-search and Sweep.
1 Heavy T.M.	do.	LA PETITE DOUVE FARM.	10 rounds.	

At 3-30 p.m. all fire will cease for five minutes to allow of Mortars cooling.

File
(app. XC)

AMENDMENT TO OPERATION ORDER NO.1.

22-9-16.

With reference to Operation Order No.1. for paragraph 8 substitute the following:-

"On the Gas Alarm being given, should the gas cloud be unaccompanied by an infantry attack, no S.O.S. signal will be sent but the Message "Gas Attack, Trench____".

The troops in the front trenches will open a slow rate of fire, rifle and machine gun, at once on against the German trenches. All howitzers should be turned on to the enemy's trenches from which the gas is being emmittd or in which the enemy infantry may be concentrating for the assault, and a light barrage by 18-pdrs. put on in NO MAN'S LAND to prevent hostile patrols from following up the gas. No intense S.O.S. barrage will be employed at this stage.

Should an infantry attack develop the normal procedure of S.O.S. will be carried out."

2nd Lieut. R.F.A.
for Adjt. 172nd Bde. R.F.A.

Copies to.
1. File
2. Diary.
3. O.C. A/172.
4. O.C. B/172.
5. O.C. D/172.
6. B.M. 36th Div. Arty.
7. B.M. 108th Inf. Bde.

Instructions regarding War Diaries and Intelligence Summaries are contained in F. S. Regs., Part II. and the Staff Manual respectively. Title Pages will be prepared in manuscript.

WAR DIARY
or
~~INTELLIGENCE~~ SUMMARY
(Erase heading not required.)

Army Form C. 2118.

Place	Date	Hour	Summary of Events and Information	Remarks and references to Appendices
In the Field	24.9.16		Very quiet. Beautiful weather. - Warm sunshine - no rain - wind dangerous	
	25.9.16		Capt. Sebag Montefiore carried out reconnaissance for Defence Scheme accompanied by the orderly officer. Beautiful weather - wind shifty, still dangerous. Enemy very quiet	Thr
	26.9.16		Hostile planes over at an early hour. A.A. guns fire without apparent success. Capt. Pitt selects position for wire cutting battery in hedge West of Artillery House. Report received of Capture of THIEPVAL & COMBLES. Weather beautiful	Thr
	27.9.16		Capt. Sebag-Montefiore in conjunction with Infantry Brigadier arranged artillery co-operation for intended raid on Brigade front (108th). At about 6 pm German captive balloon which had broken adrift passed over from direction of ARMENTIERES heavily shelled by our A.A. guns & severely damaged, was finally brought down in flames by our aircraft close to KEMMEL. One Observer killed (reported) & the other captured. Shower of rain about 12 noon - otherwise weather good. Wind from the South a little stronger, still dangerous. Operation Order No. 4 issued (appendix XI)	Thr App XI
	28.9.16		Trench Mortar Bombardment of ONTARIO FARM by our 2" trench mortars assisted by 108th Stokes mortars & 18 pdrs & 4.5" How. Commenced at 9 a.m. & continued with two breaks of 15 minutes till 10.30 a.m. Result apparently successful - otherwise normal. Weather fine with slight showers. Wind dangerous. A & B Batteries registered in connection with Group O.O. No. 5	Thr
	29.9.16		A Battery & B Battery made a demonstration of registering on WULVERGHEM-MESSINES Rd. to deceive enemy. Enemy's attitude passive. Wind dangerous. Weather dull with light rain in morning. Orders received reference formation of "Simpson's Group". O.O. No. 5 issued (app: XII) app I to O.O. No 5 issued (app: XIII)	Thr App XII & XIII

2449 Wt. W14957/M90 750,000 1/16 J.B.C. & A. Forms/C.2118/12.

Army Form C. 2118.

WAR DIARY
or
~~INTELLIGENCE~~ SUMMARY

(Erase heading not required.)

Instructions regarding War Diaries and Intelligence Summaries are contained in F. S. Regs., Part II. and the Staff Manual respectively. Title Pages will be prepared in manuscript.

Place	Date	Hour	Summary of Events and Information	Remarks and references to Appendices
In the Field	30.9.16		Trench Mortar Conference in the morning. Operation Order No. 5 cancelled at 9.30 pm owing to serious bomb accident which took place whilst issuing bombs to Raiding Party. Weather bright & warm - no rain. Enemy's attitude passive.	[illegible]

[illegible] Capt RFA
Comdg 172nd Bde RFA

2449 Wt. W14957/M90 750,000 1/16 J.B.C. & A. Forms/C.2118/12.

App. XI

Operation Order No.4.

By

Capt. T.H.Sebag-Montefiore for

Officer Commanding RIGHT GROUP.

::::::::::::::::::::::::::

Ref. Map. PLOEGSTEERT 1/10,000 — 27th. September, 1916.

1. A bombardment by the 2" Trench Mortars, of ONTARIO FARM will be carried out on Thursday, September 28th. 1916.

2. The following Units will take part:-

A/172.	18 pdr. Battery (3 guns)
D/172	4.5" How: Battery (2 guns)
Z/36	2" Trench Mortar Battery (3 guns)
108th.	Light T.M.Battery.

Tasks as per attached schedule.

The Centre and Left Groups will also take part.

3. The Operation will commence at 9.0 a.m.

4. Watches will be synchronized at 8 a.m.

5. D/172 Battery will cover the Trench Mortars while registering. Times will be arranged by O.C."D" Battery 172nd. Bde. and S.O., 36th. Div. T.M.Bs.

E.N.P. Simpson 2/Lt. R.F.A.

27.9.1916. — for Adjt.172nd. Bde. R.F.A.

Copies to

1. 36th. Div. Arty.
2. B.M.108th. Inf. Bde.
3. A/172.
4. B/172.
5. D/172.
6. Z/36 T.M.Bty.
7. 108th. Light T.M.Bty.
8. T.M.O.
9. War Diary.
10.11.& 12 File.

Battery Tasks.

A/172. (3 guns)	9.0 - 9.15 a.m.	) One gun)Hostile Support)Trench U.1.a.4593)to O.31.c.7700.	100 rounds.
	9.35-9.50 a.m.	) One Gun)Reserve Trench)O.31.c.4005 to)O.31.c.8203 and	
	10.10-10.25 a.m.	)One gun enfilades)Front Line U.1.a.)6162 to O.31.c.8203	
D/172. (2 guns)	do.	Following points:- U.1.a.4575 U.1.a.4593 U.1.a.5487 O.31.c.8203.	100 rounds
X/36 T.M.Bty.	do.	U.1.a.3962	1 round per gun per minute.
108th.Stokes Mortars	do.		5 rounds per gun per minute

Operation Order No.5.
By
Capt. T.H.Sebag-Montefiore for
Officer Commanding RIGHT GROUP

::::::::::::::::::::::

Ref.Map. Ploegsteert 1/10,000 — 28.9.1916.

1. A Raid will be carried out in the Left Sub-Sector on a date and time which will be notified later.

A, B and D Batteries will take part.

2. No preliminary bombardment is required.

3. Wire will be cut by hand or Bangalore Torpedo.

4. Alternative 1.

At 0. when the entry will be made a box barrage will be employed.

Alternative 2.

In the event of the raiding party being unable to effect an entry at first, they will telephone back before Zero time and at 0. a barrage will be put on the front and support lines; at 0.5 the box barrage will be employed.

5. The point of entry will be at U.2.c.5395 and the raiders will work left to the point of attack U.2.a.4505.

6. Ammunition allotment will be :-

750 rounds per 18 pdr. Battery
300 rounds per 4.5" How: Bty.

7. The box barrage will be continued until the order to stop is received through the Group via the Infantry. This is unlikely to be longer than 45 minutes after Zero, but in case no stop signal is received, a very slow rate of fire will be maintained.

8. Group Headquarters will be in direct telephonic communication with the Infantry. Should Alternative 2 be found necessary a priority message will be sent by the Group "Alternative two". Lines to Group H.Q. will be kept clear from one hour before zero to the stop signal.

9. Zero time will be notified. Watches will be synchronized one hour before zero.

10. A bombardment table is attached.

E.V.P. Simpson 2/Lt. R.F.A.
for Adjt.172nd. Bde.R.F.A

Copies to
1. Div.Arty. 2.B.M.108th. Inf. Bde.
3. A/172. 4.B/172.
5. D/172. 6.War Diary.
7. 11 R.I.R. 8. File.

Bombardment Table.

A/172.	<u>Alternative 1.</u> 0.0 to 0.45	4 guns search & sweep trenches 25 yards right and left of hedge running from U.2.a.2423 to U.2.a.5241. 2 guns on support line U.2.a.6817 to U.2.a. 5241 (with H.E.)	3 rounds per gun per minute for 30 minutes. 2 rounds per gun per minute for 15 minutes, then very slow rate of fire.
	<u>Alternative 2</u> 0.0. to 0.5	Barrage on front line from U.2.a.4500 to U.2.a.2431 and support line from U.2.a.6817 to U.2.a.5241.	do.
	0.5. to 0.45	As for Alternative 1.	xx.
B/172.	<u>Alternative 1.</u> 0.0. to 0.45	2 guns on front line from U.2.c.8271 to U.2.c.6584. 1 gun enfilades trench from U.2.c.7081 to U.2.c.8690. 3 guns on support line from U.2.c.9085 to U.2.a.6817 (with H.E.)	do.
	<u>Alternative2.</u> 0.0. to 0.5	Barrage on front line from U.2.c.8271 to U.2.a.4500 and support line from U.2.c.9085 to U.2.a.6817.	do.
	0.5 to 0.45	As for Alternative 1.	
D/172.	<u>Alternative 1</u> 0.0 to 0.45 or <u>Alternative 2.</u> 0.0. to 0.5 0.5. to 0.45	Will block the following points:- U.2.c.9070 U.2.a.9505 U.2.a.5342 U.2.a.2431.	2 rounds per gun per minute for 30 minutes 1 round per gun per minute for 15 minutes.

Appendix 1 to Operation Order No.5.
::::::::::::::::::::

abp XIII

The Artillery Liaison Officer for Left Sector will be with C.O. 11th. R.I.R. at O.1.d.9.5 during the course of the operations.

C.M.P. Simpson
2/Lt. R.F.A.
for Adjt.172nd. Bde.R.F.A.

29.9.1916.

Copies to
1. Div.Arty. 2. H.Q.108th. Inf.Bde.
3. A/172. 4. B/172.
5. D/172. 6. War Diary.
7. 11th R.I.R. 8. File.

Instructions regarding War Diaries and Intelligence Summaries are contained in F. S. Regs., Part II. and the Staff Manual respectively. Title Pages will be prepared in manuscript.

WAR DIARY
or
~~INTELLIGENCE SUMMARY~~
(Erase heading not required.)

Army Form C. 2118

172nd Bde RFA Vol 11

Place	Date	Hour	Summary of Events and Information	Remarks and references to Appendices
In the field	1.10.16		Very quiet day. Capt Montefiore came to live at H.Q. & take over command of Brigade. Col Ward goes on leave. Weather overcast but no rain.	Ibh
	2.10.16		Enemy attitude passive. Capt. Montefiore in company with Lt Beavis. D.T.M.O visited front line trenches for the purpose of selecting defensive positions for Trench mortars. Positions also decided upon for forthcoming bombardment of enemy wire & front line. Acting O.C. Bde also visited Battalion & Coy. H.Q. & tested communication. Two test rounds fired. Weather - heavy & continuous rain set in about 11 am till evening. D/172 vacate their position under Hill 63 and take up position near KEMMEL on detached duty as one of the batteries of "Simpson's Group". Wind round to S.W. reported safe. Centre Group lend 2 howitzers for defence of line.	Ibh
	3.10.16		Enemy attitude continues passive. All conditions normal. Anzac Corps Horse Show in the afternoon. Weather overcast, showery, but improved in the afternoon. Wind still safe. Visited A & B Batteries' Wagon lines. A/172 firing evening fire to Z36 T.M. Bty co-operating with Stokes on ONTARIO FARM.	Ibh
	4.10.16		Enemy reported shelling STINKING FARM about 1 pm. A & B Batteries ordered to retaliate by shelling farm & other buildings in and behind MESSINES. Effect: enemy cease fire at once. Acting O.C. Bde makes reconnaissance with Staff Captain for position of wagon line of new Howitzer Battery whose arrival at HAVRE is reported. Weather overcast with heavy showers. Wind safe. 60 pdr. Battery on our left very active between 9 pm & 10 pm. Visited A & B Battery positions & D Battery Wagon line	Ibh

1875 Wt. W593/826 1,000,000 4/15 J.B.C. & A. A.D.S.S./Forms/C. 2118.

Instructions regarding War Diaries and Intelligence Summaries are contained in F. S. Regs., Part II. and the Staff Manual respectively. Title Pages will be prepared in manuscript.

WAR DIARY
or
~~INTELLIGENCE SUMMARY~~
(Erase heading not required.)

Army Form C. 2118

Place	Date	Hour	Summary of Events and Information	Remarks and references to Appendices
In the Field	5.10.16		at 8.30 am combined TM & Artillery bombardment carried out on 108th Inf. Bde. front. Very successful Z.36 T.M.Bty do very good work from temporary positions in front line. Viewed operations from A Battery OP. at 11.30 am met CRA & DTMO at HYDE PARK CORNER and went round HTM & MTM positions, offensive & defensive in 108th Bde area. Issued operation orders No(7) for gas attack at 1 am night 5/6th oct. Cancelled at 11 pm (appendix I)	appendix I.
	6.10.16		Visited A & B Battery Wagon lines in the morning & A & B Battery gun positions in the afternoon. Very little artillery action. Weather fine & dry. O.O. No.6. issued. (appendix II)	app: II
	7.10.16		2 m Conference at Centre front H2 at 10.30 am. Programme for next week discussed & settled. Visited Col Blacker 9th RIF. & settled details of Artillery co-operation in raid arranged for 12th inst.. Visited ADVS at Bailleul & discussed winter stable management. Z 36 T.M.Bty fired 60 rds on ONTARIO FARM covered by A.172. 529th How Bty arrived at Bailleul from Havre at 11 pm	
	8.10.16		529th Howitzer Battery settled in temporary wagon line near No 1 Section DAC. at 4 am. Visited them in the morning and also A & B wagon lines. Visited A Battery gun line in afternoon. Major Bolitho returns from leave having spent 2 days in No.7 at Boulogne. OO No.8 issued. (app: III)	app: III
	9.10.16		Capt. Montefiore hands over to Major Bolitho. Date of Raid altered to 11th. Visited 529th Bty arranged for this Battery to move to DRANOUTRE. Inspected B Battery Wagon line & gun position	

Army Form C. 2118.

WAR DIARY
or
~~INTELLIGENCE~~ SUMMARY
(Erase heading not required.)

Instructions regarding War Diaries and Intelligence Summaries are contained in F. S. Regs., Part II. and the Staff Manual respectively. Title Pages will be prepared in manuscript.

Place	Date	Hour	Summary of Events and Information	Remarks and references to Appendices
In the Field	10.10.16		Conferred with 108th Inf. Bde re Scheme for raid. Discussed scheme for raid with C.R.A. Scheme was considerably altered. Explained new artillery arrangement for raid to O.C. 9th R.I.F. who expressed himself satisfied.	[initials]
	11.10.16		529th Battery moved to DRANOUTRE. Inspected 529th Battery's arrangements. 2.0 am 11-12th raid carried out on enemy's trenches at LA PETITE DOUVE. Raid reported unsuccessful. Artillery reported to have carried out programme correctly & satisfactorily. Lt Col. Ward returned from leave 8.0 am & resumed command. O.O. No. 9 issued (appendix IV)	[initials] app: IV
	12.10.16		Visited 529th Battery at DRANOUTRE & inspected the horses & sites for standings etc. Authority received that 529th Battery would in future become C/172. Weather very windy	[initials]
	13.10.16		Visited battery positions A. B & D. & wagon line of D during the morning & wagon lines A & B during the afternoon. Day quiet on the whole. H.Q. horse lines completed. Weather windy raw & overcast	
	14.10.16		Conference ~~with~~ at H.Q. 153rd Bde. Visited front O.Ps in the afternoon. Z36 T.M.Bty fixed up to allotment during the morning. Weather - cloudy, cold but no rain.	[initials]
	15.10.16		Conference with O.C. Z.36 T.M.Bty. Trench Mortar Operation Orders No. 3 issued (appendix V)	app: V
	16.10.16		Inspected trench mortar positions including Heavy T.M. & Fabian Farm. Visited Company Headquarters in front line & tested both 18 pdrs. battery communications also inspected camouflage O.P. in trench U.11 bay 9. Visited both battalion Headquarters. In the afternoon visited C/172 at Dranoutre & inspected their horses. Weather fine & sunny, but cold	[initials]

2449 Wt. W14957/M90 750,000 1/16 J.B.C. & A. Forms/C.2118/12.

WAR DIARY
or
~~INTELLIGENCE~~ SUMMARY

(*Erase heading not required.*)

Army Form C. 2118.

Instructions regarding War Diaries and Intelligence Summaries are contained in F. S. Regs., Part II. and the Staff Manual respectively. Title Pages will be prepared in manuscript.

Place	Date	Hour	Summary of Events and Information	Remarks and references to Appendices
In the Field	17.10.16		During the morning visited OP U.14 with OC A/172 battery and also visited Wagon line D/172. Trench Mortar OO No 3 commenced at 3.55pm. For ten minutes the Stokes + 2" TMs made good practice, but hostile artillery found them and very soon put both natures out of action. The 2" TMs managed to fire 23 rounds but one gun was knocked out and the other drove its bed into the soft ground. There were two casualties in the Stokes Battery. The heavy T.M. fired well with fair accuracy - some rounds were however short. The artillery bombardment was well carried out. The dominating position of MESSINES RIDGE renders the use of 2" TMs + Stokes TMs a dangerous operation the results of which are not commensurate with the raids. Weather overcast - glooming + cold.	-
	18.10.16		all group orders + arrangements brought up to date + revised for record. (app: VI) Visited Wagon line C/172 at DRANOUTRE. Weather overcast - rain + cold.	app: VI
	19.10.16		C.R.A came + discussed question of TM positions for proposed raid made out + issued. OO No 10 issued (app: VIII) conference with Major Hardy RE + OC Z 36 T.M.Bty on subject of 2" TM positions. Inspected billets of Z 36 T.M.Bty. Weather wet + cold	app: VIII
	20.10.16		Visited A.B + C batteries to communicate G.O.C.R.A letter on subject of short rounds - also made inspection of all these positions. Z 36 T.M.Bty. cut wire at U.1.d. 20.58 during morning of 19th result reported good. During afternoon visited OPs of A + D Batts + reconnoitred scene of proposed raid. Weather bright, clear + cold.	

2449 Wt. W14957/M90 750,000 1/16 J.B.C. & A. Forms/C.2118/12.

Army Form C. 2118.

Instructions regarding War Diaries and Intelligence Summaries are contained in F. S. Regs., Part II. and the Staff Manual respectively. Title pages will be prepared in manuscript.

WAR DIARY
or
~~INTELLIGENCE~~ SUMMARY.

(Erase heading not required.)

Place	Date	Hour	Summary of Events and Information	Remarks and references to Appendices
In the Field	21.10.16		Weekly Conference. During afternoon visited both battalion commanders in the line at the Bn. H.Q. 2" T.M.s carried out wire cutting & expended 79 rounds with good result. Weather – bright – north wind – very cold & bracing	[illegible]
	22.10.16		Visited defensive positions for G.H.Q. 2nd line & 3rd line & B Battery wagon line. O.C. 41st Heavy Group came in the afternoon & discussed question of ammunition for D/172. Weather fine – bright – but very cold. A quiet day very little activity.	[illegible]
	23.10.16		Made tour of trenches accompanied by T.M. officer. Inspected all sites for proposed T.M. positions permanent & semi-permanent, & sites for men's dug-outs. Also visited Company Headquarters & tested their artillery communications. During the afternoon visited wagon line of C/172 & inspected wagon line of A.172. Weather fine – but milder.	
	24.10.16		Visited battery position & O.P. of D/172 battery with O.C. 41st Heavy Group. Also visited battery position B/172. In afternoon presented ribbons of Military Medal to Sgt. MacCormack & Gunner Roffey. Examined 2/Lt. M.B.R.A. D.A.S. in gunnery. Weather wet & raw.	[illegible]
	25.10.16		G.O.C. 36th Division inspected wagon line of A & B Batt. in the morning. Weather – wet & cold. Z.36 T.M. Bty. expended 69 rounds on wire cutting	[illegible]
	26.10.16		Visited both Battn. Headquarters in the morning & inspected the horse-standing C/172 during the afternoon. Weather cleared & became fine – & sunny but rather cold.	[illegible]

2353 Wt. W2544/1454 700,000 5/15 D. D. & L. A.D.S.S./Forms/C. 2118.

Instructions regarding War Diaries and Intelligence Summaries are contained in F. S. Regs., Part II. and the Staff Manual respectively. Title pages will be prepared in manuscript.

WAR DIARY

or

~~INTELLIGENCE~~ SUMMARY.

(Erase heading not required.)

Army Form C. 2118.

Place	Date	Hour	Summary of Events and Information	Remarks and references to Appendices
In the Field.	27.10.16		accompanied C.R.A in tour of inspection of all trench mortar emplacements & dug-outs. Visited wagon line C/172. Weather - cloudy - overcast & cold - showery	[initials]
	28.10.16		Weekly Conference. Inspected D/172 wagon line - Z.36. T.M. Battery bombarded hostile front line from 11.30 am to 12.30 pm. B/172 & D/172 providing covering fire. Visited positions selected by B/172 & D/172 for defence of subsidiary line. Weather overcast - showery - not quite so cold. Capt. A.E.S.M. Callis command of A/172 Battery vice Captain J.H. Sebag-Montefiore transferred to T. Batt. R.H.A.	[initials]
	29.10.16		operation orders No 11 issued (app. VIII) Visited battery position of A/172. Weather windy - showery & cold.	app VIII [initials]
	30.10.16		Inspected battery position D/172. Weather very wet & windy - both artilleries very quiet. observation too bad for action	[initials]
	31.10.16		Visited both battalion commanders in the line - also inspected work done on dug-outs by Z.36 T.M.Bty & their semi-permanent positions & OP in Rome Street. also inspected emplacement of heavy T.M. In afternoon went to C/172 wagon line at ORANOUTRE and inspected horses & horse lines. Weather windy & cold - some heavy showers - but greatly improved	[initials]

L. E. S. Ward Lt Col RFA
Comdg 172nd Bde RFA

2353 Wt. W2544/1454 700,000 5/15 D. D. & L. A.D.S.S./Forms/C. 2118.

OPERATION ORDER NO. 7.

by

Captain T.H. Jebb-Montefiore, R.F.A.,

Commanding Right Group Artillery.

[illegible]

Ref Map. [illegible] 1/10,000.

1\. The Gas Cylinders installed in all three Brigade Sectors will be discharged tonight if weather conditions are favourable.

Zero Time will be at an hour to be notified later.

The Gas will be discharged at full density from 0 to 15 minutes, and will then cease altogether.

If at any time prior to the hour of discharge, the conditions are considered definately unfavourable, the following telegram will be sent from this Office:-

"The answer is No".

This will cancel the attack.

2\. From 0.4 to 0.25 [illegible] batteries will bombard points as laid down in the attached list of tasks.

[illegible] rounds per battery will be allowed, which will come out of the present allotment.

The enemy's front line and support line on the front of the Gas Attack will be bombarded by Medium and Light Trench Mortars.

3\. Patrols will be out from 1 hour and 15 minutes after Zero, and will endeavour to investigate the effects of the Gas.

4\. Signal time will be sent out at [illegible] p.m. and 8 p.m.

From 8 p.m. all wires will be reserved for tactical purposes.

5\. No information or instructions regarding these operations will be sent by telephone or telegraph, except in code.

W.A. [illegible]

2nd Lieut. R.F.A.,

Adjt. 173rd Bde. R.F.A.

Copies to.

1\. 36 Div. Arty. [illegible] 108th Inf. Bde.

3\. A/173. 4. B/173.

5\. X 36 T.M. Baty. 6. [illegible]

7\. War Diary. 9. File.

9\. D/153. 10. Centre Group.

Table of Tasks.

A/172. 2 guns will spray with shrapnel, road [support] and communication trenches between O.32.c.3218 - O.32.c.7510 - U.2.a.4575.

3 guns on Support trenches between U.2.a.5475 and U.2.a.8005.

1 gun will shell Platoon Dug-Outs about O.33.a.43.

B/172. 1 gun will shell support trench from U.2.a.8005 to U.2.c.9075.

2 guns will shell support trench from U.2.d.4777 to U.8.b.2285.

2 guns from U.8.b.2285 to U.8.b.5022.

1 gun will shell road and Platoon Dug-Outs about O.33.c.94.

D/153. (One Section)
2 Hows: will bombard the Battalion Hd.Qrs. and approaches thereto at O.[illegible]3.d.76 and U.2.b.2012.

Rates of fire. 18 pdrs.
3 rds. per gun per minute for 4 mins:
1 rd. do. do. for 12 do.
2 rds. do. do. for 5 do.
(~~[illegible]~~ 4 mins, all shrapnel will be used)

Howitzers.
50 rds. per gun (Total 100 rds)

Appendix 1. to Right Group

Operation Order No.7.

::::::::::::::::::::::::

Zero Time at 1.0 a.m.

Z/[illegible]th. Trench Mortar Battery will not take part in the operations but will assist Y/[illegible]th. Trench Mortar Battery if required.

W.A. [illegible] (signature)

[illegible] R.F.A.
Adjt.17[illegible]nd. [illegible]

[illegible].11.1916.

Copies to
1. [illegible] Div. Arty.
2. [illegible] Inf. Bde.
3. [illegible]/172.
4. D/172.
5. [illegible]
6. [illegible]
7. [illegible]
8. File.
9. [illegible]
10. Centre Group.

app: II

Operation Order No. [illegible]

by

Capt. [illegible] Sebag-Montefiore R.F.A.

Commanding [illegible] Group.

::::::::::::::::::::::::::::

Ref. Map. [illegible] 4th October, 1916.

1. A bombardment of the enemy's line between [illegible] to [illegible] will be carried out by the Right Group in conjunction with [illegible] on Thursday, 5th instant, beginning at [illegible] a.m.

2. The following time table will be observed:-

[illegible] a.m.	- [illegible] a.m.	Bombardment.
[illegible] a.m.	- [illegible] a.m.	Interval.
[illegible] a.m.	- [illegible] a.m.	Bombardment.
[illegible] a.m.	- [illegible] a.m.	Silent.
[illegible] a.m.	- [illegible] a.m.	Bombardment.

Signal time will be sent out at [illegible] a.m.

3. The following units will take part:-

[illegible]/172.
[illegible]/172.
One Section [illegible]/167.
[illegible] 36th. [illegible]
108th. Inf. Bde. Stokes [illegible]

Tasks as per attached schedule.

[illegible] (signature)
Major R.F.A.
Comdg. 172nd. Bde. R.F.A.

4.10.1916.

Copies to

1. 36th. Div. Arty.
2. [illegible] Inf. Bde.
3. Centre Group.
4. [illegible]/172.
5. [illegible]/172.
6. [illegible]/153.
7. [illegible] 36th. [illegible]
8. 108th. Inf. Bde. ([illegible]) [illegible]
9. [illegible]
10. War Diary.
11. File.

T A S K S .

A/172.	One gun on hostile support line from U.2.a.5111 to U.2.a.4225. Two Sections on hostile support line from U.2.a.7017 to U.2.a.5045.	One round per gun per minute. (150 rds.total)
B/172.	Three guns on hostile support line from U.2.c.8791 to U.2.a.7017 One Section enfilade communication trenches running from U.2.c.7180 to U.2.c.8791 U.2.c.8099 to U.2.b.3613.	One round per gun per minute. (150 rds. total)
D/153.	Following points:- U.2.a.5113. U.2.a.5007.	75 rounds total. 25 rds. for each period.
Z 36th. T.M.Bty.	Will bombard the following area:- U.2.c.5096. U.2.a.4205. U.2.a.5113. U.2.c.5398.	1 round per gun per minute.
108th.(Stokes) Mortars.	Will bombard same area as Z 36th. T.M.Bty.	6 rounds per gun per minute.

App. III

OPERATION ORDER NO. 8.

by

Captain T.M. Sebag-Montefiore, R.F.A.,

Commanding Right Group Artillery.

Ref. Map. PLOEGSTEERT 1/10,000. 8-10-16.

The Right Group, 36th Divisional Artillery will search "NO MAN'S LAND" with shrapnel fire in the hope of catching enemy patrols, in accordance with the following programme.

Night 8th and 9th instant. 7-30 p.m. to 7-35 p.m. and
7-40 p.m. to 7-45 p.m.

B/172. LA PETITE DOUVE FARM.

A/172. "NO MAN'S LAND" from STINKING FARM - MESSINES ROAD to U.2.a.0505.

Night 9th and 10th instant. 12-30 a.m. to 12-35 a.m. and
12-40 a.m. to 12-45 a.m.

B/172. "NO MAN'S LAND" from U.2.c.5050 to U.2.a.2000.

A/172. "NO MAN'S LAND" from U.2.a.2000 to U.2.a.0040.

Night 10th and 11th instant. No firing will take place.

Night 11th and 12th instant. 10 p.m. to 10-5 p.m. and
10-10 p.m. to 10-15 p.m.

B/172. "NO MAN'S LAND" from U.2.a.1000 to U.1.b.8070.

A/172. "NO MAN'S LAND" from U.1.b.8070 to O.31.d.7020.

Ammunition:- 16 rounds per battery per night will be fired.

W A [signature]
2nd Lieut. R.F.A.,
Adjt. 172nd Bde. R.F.A.

Copies to:-
1 36th Div. Arty.
2 B.M. 108th Inf. Bde.
3 A/172.
4 B/172.
5 War Diary.
6 File.

app. IV

Operation Order No.9. Copy No.______

By

Major E.W.Bolitho R.F.A.,

Commanding RIGHT GROUP

::::::::::::::::::::::

Ref. Map. PLOEGSTEERT 1/10,000 11th. October, 1916.

1. A raid will be carried out in the Right Sub-Sector on Petite Douve Farm on the night of the 11th/12th instant.

A/172.
B/172
D/172.
Z36th. T.M.Bty.
Corps Heavy Artillery.

Will take part.

ZERO time will be 2 a.m.

2. Wire will be cut by a Bangalore Torpedo.

3. Point of entry U.8.a.8867.

4. A bombardment in U.2.c.will take place with a view to silencing the large number of machine guns known to exist here and if necessary the M.T.M. of U.2.c.8080.

5. Time of entry +18.

6. From Zero to +3 — No Man's Land in front of Petite Douve will be sprinkled with shrapnel and Stokes Mortars with the object of driving in enemy patrols and posts holding Sap Heads.

+8 to +18 — An intensive bombardment on Petite Douve and Communication Trenches. T.M's will fire from +8 to +11 and +14 to +17.

+18 to stop signal — Box barrage will be put on by 18 pdr.batteries.

7. The Artillery Liaison Officer of the Right Sub-Sector will be with the Bn. Commander in the Right Coy. H.Q. and will be responsible for communicating all information to the Right Group Commander.

8. Ammunition required - 276 rounds per 18 pdr. Battery. 200 rounds per 4.5" Howitzer Battery. 16 per 2" Trench Mortar Battery.

9. Table of tasks attached.

10. ACKNOWLEDGE.

W.A. Stevenson
2/Lt. R.F.A.
Adjt.172nd. Bde. R.F.A.

Copies to

1. File.
2. Diary.
3. A/172.
4. B/172.
5. D/172.
6. Z36th. T.M.Bty.
7. 108th. Stokes Mortars.
8. B.M.36th. Div. Arty.
10. B.M.108th. Inf. Bde.
11. D.T.M.O.

Tasks.

0 to +3	B/172.	Will sprinkle "No Man's Land" from U.8.a.8040 to U.8.a.8060.
	A/172.	Will sprinkle from U.8.a.8061 to U.8.a.8080
		1 round per gun per minute, total per Bty. 18¼
+8 to +18	B/172.	5 guns will bombard U.8.b.0038 to U.8.a.8867 1 gun on U.8.b.0759.
	A/172.	5 guns will bombard U.8.a.8867 to U.8.b.1294 1 gun on U.8.b.0977.
		Two rounds per gun per minute, total per Bty 120 rds.
	D/172.	One gun on U.8.b.4040. One gun on U.8.b.2288. Two guns on Machine Guns known to exist in the neighbourhood of U.2.c.7080.
		(if 6" Hows: are available they will fire on these machine guns relieving the latter of D/172 who will then fire on U.8.b.2041 and U.8.b.3366.
		1 round per gun per minute, total 40 rounds.
+8 to +11 and +14 to +17.	236th. T.M.Bty.	Will bombard the point of entry and 50 yards on either flank.
+11 to +14		Silence.

Box Barrage.

+18 to +40	B/172.	1 gun on U.8.a.9240. 1 gun on U.8.b.1040. 1 gun on U.8.b.3042. 2 guns from U.8.b.4040 to U.8.b.3065, both points exclusive. 1 gun on U.8.b.1892.
	A/172.	4 guns from U.8.b.3065 to U.8.b.2288, both points exclusive. 2 guns on U.8.b.1090.
		+18 to +23 1rd. per gun per minute. Total per Bty. 30. +23 to +29 2 rds. do. do. Total per Bty. 72. +28 to +40 1 rd. do. 2 minute Total per Bty. 36.
	D/172.	As above. +18 to +33 2rds. per gun per minute. Total 120 rds. +33 to +40 1 rd. do. do. Total 28 rds.
	T.M's	Silent.

Appendix 1 to Right Group Operation

Order No.9.

:::::::::

Table of tasks. Box Barrage.

-18 to 140. B/172 will not fire their one gun on U.8.b.1892 but will fire on U.8.a.9622 and will sweep 40 yards. A/172 will fire 3 guns instead of 4 guns on U.8.b.30 3065 to U.8.b.2288, the 4th. gun will fire on U.8.b.1892.

2/Lt. R.F.A.
Adjt.172nd. Bde.

11.10.1916.

36

Vol 12

Army Form C. 2118.

Instructions regarding War Diaries and Intelligence Summaries are contained in F. S. Regs., Part II. and the Staff Manual respectively. Title pages will be prepared in manuscript.

WAR DIARY
or
~~INTELLIGENCE SUMMARY.~~
(Erase heading not required.)

172nd Bde. RFA

Place	Date	Hour	Summary of Events and Information	Remarks and references to Appendices
In the Field	1.11.16		Inspected wagon lines & horses of A B & C Batteries. Operations commenced in accordance with OO/101 at 7 pm & time table was accurately carried out. Raid failed owing to raiding party coming on unexpected & very strong wire. No casualties to personnel & equipment. Weather fine & cold	[illegible]
	2.11.16		Greater part of the day spent at 2nd Army Trench Mortar School – lecture on 2"TM & 9.45. Weather showery in the morning – fine in the afternoon – much colder.	[illegible]
	3.11.16		Inspected battery positions A B & D & wagon lines C & D. Weather – no rain – milder.	[illegible]
	4.11.16		Watched trench mortar bombardment from O.P. 'B' Battery. A B & D Batts gave covering fire. Trench mortars not very effective – several rounds plus. Inspected alternative O.Ps U.13.014 & U.17. A.D.V.S. inspected horses & reported them in good condition. Weather – fine & mild	[illegible]
	5.11.16		Visited battery positions A & B. Weather – no rain but very windy & cold. App. IV to Precis of Arrangements (appendix I) issued. Appen. V to Precis of Arrangements issued (app. II).	app. I app. II
	6.11.16		Made tour of T.M. positions and dug-outs and saw both battalion commanders. Met drainage expert at A172 position. Heavy showers & cold	[illegible]
	7.11.16		Compiled & issued memorandum on defence scheme 108th Infantry Bde front. Weather very hard – heavy rain almost continuously throughout the day. App. VI to Precis of Arrangements issued (app. III)	app. III
	8.11.16		Inspected horses & wagon lines of all Batteries – horses of A172 not very satisfactory. Trenches in right sub sector flooded by river Douve rising. Orders received to assume a passive attitude. Liaison officer detailed for Right Bat. H.Q. Slight improvement in weather but some heavy showers fell	[illegible]

A5834 Wt. W4973/M687 750,000 8/16 D. D. & L. Ltd. Forms/C.2118/13.

Instructions regarding War Diaries and Intelligence Summaries are contained in F. S. Regs., Part II. and the Staff Manual respectively. Title pages will be prepared in manuscript.

WAR DIARY
or
~~INTELLIGENCE SUMMARY.~~
(Erase heading not required.)

Army Form C. 2118.

Place	Date	Hour	Summary of Events and Information	Remarks and references to Appendices
In the Field	9.11.16	–	Visited both battalion HQ + dug-outs of Z36 TM Bty – conditions in right subsector still bad but greatly improved visited battery positions A B + D. all of which had suffered from the heavy rain. Drainage of A Battery progressing well. Weather greatly improved – fine – sunny – Very good observation – colder.	Th
	10.11.16		Visited all O.Ps + inspected log + registration books. Reconnoitred four O.Ps in fire trench + found them unsuitable. Visited wagon line C/172 at Dranoutre. Weather fine + sunny – frost during the night.	Th
	11.11.16		Inspected billets of Z36 T.M. Bty in Neuve Eglise + found them satisfactory. During afternoon visited wagon lines A + B and inspected horses and accommodation. Weather overcast but no rain – temperature much milder.	Th
	12.11.16		Visited Wagon line C/172 battery. Overcast + dull – no rain – observation bad – hostile artillery activity much decreased during last three days.	Th
	13.11.16		Inspected battery positions of B + D + horses of D. A trench mortar conference was held at Bde HQ – 153 in the afternoon. OO order No 12 issued app. IV Weather fine + mild	app. IV
	14.11.16		Visited battalion headquarters right + left subsectors + company headquarters in front line, also inspected emplacement of heavy trench mortar + temporary positions of three medium trench mortars + reconnoitred tramways for use with Heavy T.M. but concluded this was not possible. Inspected A Battery position in the afternoon. Weather – no rain but cloudy + overcast – temperature colder.	Th

Army Form C. 2118.

Instructions regarding War Diaries and Intelligence Summaries are contained in F. S. Regs., Part II. and the Staff Manual respectively. Title pages will be prepared in manuscript.

WAR DIARY
or
INTELLIGENCE SUMMARY.
(Erase heading not required.)

Place	Date	Hour	Summary of Events and Information	Remarks and references to Appendices
In the Field	15.11.16		Bombardment in accordance with O.O. No 12 carried out. 2" & heavy T.M. fired very well & sustained their tasks throughout. Stokes mortars were not very effective. No artillery casualties were sustained. Visited wagon line C/172 in the afternoon. Weather frosty & cold.	[initials]
	16.11.16		Visited O.P.s & battalion H.Q. reconnoitred trench tramways for purpose of mobile trench mortars but found all unsuitable in front area. Inspected horses & wagon line "A" Battery. Weather very cold & fine - a hard frost	
	17.11.16		Visited wagon line B/172 & also inspected battery positions A & B & subsidiary line position A. In afternoon made reconnaissance of [illegible] Drive area from O.P. B/172. Weather - a fine sunny day - very good observation - heavy frost app: VII to Precis of Arrangements issued, app: V	[initials] app V
	18.11.16		Conference during the morning. Z36 T.M. Bty fired experimental series with silencer. Inspected wagon line, horses & harness B/172. Weather - hard frost in morning turned to rain.	[initials]
	19.11.16		Inspected Z36 T.M. Bty in F.S. Marching Order. During afternoon prepared scheme for Artillery action for Raid 108th Bde. Weather stormy & cold. app VII to Precis of Arrangements issued. app: VI	app VI [initials]
	20.11.16		Inspected C/172 battery in F.S. marching order & on line of march. Weather showery & cold. app IX to precis of arrangements issued (app VII)	app VII
	21.11.16		Visited all company headquarters & both battalion commanders also inspected 2" trench mortar emplacements both permanent & semi-permanent. In the afternoon inspected battery position of A & D. A very quiet day. Weather very foggy & artillery observation impossible. A hard frost at night	[initials]
	22.11.16		Visited C Battery wagon line at [illegible]. Weather cold & overcast. O.O. No. 13 issued app: VIII	app: VIII

A5834 Wt. W4973/M687 750,000 8/16 D. D. & L. Ltd. Forms/C.2118/13.

Instructions regarding War Diaries and Intelligence Summaries are contained in F. S. Regs., Part II. and the Staff Manual respectively. Title pages will be prepared in manuscript.

WAR DIARY
or
~~INTELLIGENCE SUMMARY.~~
(Erase heading not required.)

Army Form C. 2118.

Place	Date	Hour	Summary of Events and Information	Remarks and references to Appendices
In the Field	23.11.16		Visited C Battery wagon line at Dranoutre. Weather cold & overcast. Amendment to Right Group OO13 issued. app. VIII	app. IX
	24.11.16		Visited wagon line B Battery & watched section training. T.M. Bombardment Operation Order No. 13. Weather overcast, cloudy & cold.	
	25.11.16		Conference at H2 153 Bde. R.F.A., Z.36 T.M. Bty fire experimental series with silencer - very successful 48 rounds being fired. Weather - showery & cloudy - very cold.	
	26.11.16		A very quiet day - foggy & very poor observation.	
	27.11.16		Visited Battery positions of B & D. & O.Ps of A & D. Weather too misty for observation. Visited D wagon line. Artillery activity of both sides nil. Weather better but still misty, cloudy & cold.	
	28.11.16		Visited three Company HdQrs & both Battn. H2. Very misty, observation impossible	
	29.11.16		Very quiet day. Observation impossible owing to mist. Discussed scheme for dealing with hostile working parties with Infantry Bde Major.	
	30.11.16		Explained Scheme for dealing with hostile working parties to Infantry Intelligence Officers at LA PLUS DOUVE F^m. Conference with G.O.C. 2nd Army at 108th Inf. Bde H2.	

L. E. S. Ward Lt Col RFA
Comdg 172nd Bde RFA

A5834 Wt. W4973/M687 750,000 8/16 D. D. & L. Ltd. Forms/C.2118/13.

app I

Appendix to Precis of Arrangements

RIGHT GROUP.
::::::::

Instructions for Trench Mortars:-

S.O.S.	V 36th. H.T.M.Bty.	One gun fires on U.8.a.9572
	Z 36th. T.M.Bty. (2inch)	All guns in action. Barrage from U.1.b.8732 to U.2.a.0510

Defensive Measures.

If circumstances necessitate a withdrawal from our present front line 2" Trench Mortars will be established at the following points:-

W.A.E. U.7.b.6070 firing on zone from U.8.a.4548 to U.2.c.1039

U.1.c.9040 firing on zone from U.2.c.1039 to U.1.b.1035

Heavy Trench Mortar at U.7.b.6049 will fire on front line trench from U.2.c.2320 to U.8.a.4525.

W.A. Edmenson.
Lt & Adjt.
172nd. Brigade. R.F.A.

5.11.1916.

Copies to

1. B.M.36th.Div.Arty.
2. A/172.
3. B/172.
4. D/172.
5. C/172.
6. Z 36th. T.M.Bty.
7. V 36th.T.M.Bty.
8. D.T.M.O.
9. File
10. Diary.

App. II

Appendix 5 to Precis of Arrangements

RIGHT GROUP.

::::::

RED HAND Signal.

This Signal if sent by telephone or buzzer will be followed by the number of the Trench which is being bombarded; e.g. "RED HAND N.36.4 " It will be an "Urgent Priority" call and will be preceded by the Stop Signal.

Artillery Preparation.

By Day. All guns are laid on Communication Trenches, and Trench Junctions as far back as the Support Line inclusive, this being the probable area in which the enemy will assemble for attack.

A large proportion of H.E. will be used.

The lines the guns are laid on will be known as "Day Lines" and guns will be on these lines from an hour after dawn until an hour before dusk. °

By Night. If the RED HAND Signal is made at night, the guns will fire on their present night lines, i.e. on the enemy's front line parapet along the whole front except in U.1.b. where they are along the valley of the STEENBEEK.

The 4.5" Howitzers fire on selected Trench Junctions.

Rate of fire.

Opening fire will be Section Fire 30 seconds on the above lines. By day this fire will be controlled according to the observations of Officers in the O.P's. and reports received from the Infantry. Group Commanders will be able to vary the rate according to circumstances.

By night the opening rate will be maintained throughout.

W A Edmenson
Lt. R.F.A.
Adjt. Right Group.

5.11.1916.

°Points on which guns are laid for the RED HAND Signal as shewn in para.3. under heading DAY LINES

Copies to

1. B.M.36th. Div. Arty.
2. A/172.
3. B/172.
4. C/172.
5. D/172.
6. Z 36th. T.M.Bty.
7. V 36th. T.M.Bty.
8. D.T.M.O.
9. File.
10. Diary.

V

Appendix VII to Precis of Arrangements

RIGHT GROUP.

:::::::

Batteries will draw their ammunition as follows and not as stated in Appendix II to Precis of Arrangements:-

No.1. Section will supply.

A/172 B/172 and D/172. Batteries.

Map Spotting T.20.c.8.9

No.2. Section will supply

C/172.

Map Spotting M.34.b.2.9

W.A. Emerson
Lt. R.F.A.
Adjt.172nd. Bde.R.F.A.

17.11.1916.

Copies as for Precis of Arrangements.

VII.

Appendix VIII to Precis of Arrangements

RIGHT GROUP.

:::::::::::

Reference Subsidiary Line Defence.

B/172 Battery has selected a new position at

T.23.b.4660.

W.A. Edmenson

Lt. R.F.A.

19.11.1916. Adjt.172nd. Bde. R.F. A

Copies as for Precis of Arrangements.

VII

Appendix IX to Precis of Arrangements

RIGHT GROUP.

<u>Gas and Red Hand</u> .

Instructions for Trench Mortars.

In the event of Gas being discharged by the enemy or the Rec Hand Signal being given you will actt as laid down for S.O.S.

W A Edmenson

Lt. R.F.A.

.20.11.1916. Adjt.172nd. Bde.

VIII

Operation Orders No.13. Copy No.________

By

Lieut. Col.L.K.S.Ward, D.S.O., R.F.A.

Commanding RIGHT GROUP.

::::::::::::

Ref. Map. PLOEGSTEERT 1/10,000 22nd. November, 1916.

1. On Friday next the 24th. instant the following points will be bombarded by Z 36th. T.M.Battery commencing at 10.30 a.m. Duration one hour.

U.2.a.3030 to) New work.
U.2.c.7090)

2. A/172)
B/172) Will give covering fire.
D/172)

3. A/172 will fire from 10.30 a.m. to 11 a.m. and B/172 from 11 a.m. to 11.30 a.m. on support and communication trenches between U.2.a.3030 and U.2.c.7090.

20 rounds AX per Battery allotted for the operation.

D/172 will fire throughout on WILLIE, WHACKER, WHY NOT, WINTER and WALLIS.

40 rounds will be allotted for the operation.

4. D/172 will be ready to turn on to any hostile T.M's that may open fire reporting immediately to Group H.Q. as per standing orders.

5. ACKNOWLEDGE.

W A Edmenson
Lt. R.F.A.
Adjt.172nd. Bde. R.F.A.

22.11.1916.

Copies to

1. B.M.36th. Div. Arty.
2. B.M.108th. Inf. Bde.
3. A/172.
4. B/172.
5. D/172.
6. Z 36th. T.M.Bty.
7. D.T.M.O.
8. File.
9. Diary.

IXI

Amendment 1 to Right Group Operation

Orders dated 22.11.1916.

:::::::::::::

18 pdr Batteries will have 30 AX allotted for the operation instead of 20 AX as stated in para.3.

W A Edmenson

Lt. R.F. A.

23.11.1916. Adjt.172nd. Bde. R.F.A.

Copies as for O.O.No.13.

Appendix VI to Precis of Arrangements

VII

RIGHT GROUP.

::::::::

Reference Subsidiary Line defence.

D/172 Battery has selected a new position at

T.23.c.09.75.

W A Edmenson

Lt. & Adjt.
172nd. Bde. R.F.A.

7.11.1916.

Copy to

1. B.M.36th. Div.Arty.
2. A/172.
3. B/172.
4. C/172.
5. D/172.
6. X 36th.T.M.Bty.
7. V 36th. T.M.Bty.
8. D.T.M.O.
9. File.
10. DIARY.
11. B.M. 108. I Bde

app IV

Operation Orders No.12. Copy No.

by

Lieut. Col. L.E.S. Ward, D.S.O., R.F.A.

Commanding RIGHT GROUP.

:::::::::::::

Ref. Map. PLOEGSTEERT 1/10,000 November 14th. 1916.

1. A combined bombardment of the hostile defences at U.2.c.6783 to U.2.c.5097 and U.8.a.8848 to U.8.a.9780 will be carried out on Wednesday 15th. instant.

The following Units will take part:-

A/172	)
B/172	) 18 pdr. Batteries.
D/172	4.5" Howitzer Battery.
Z 36th. T.M.Bty.	3 guns.
V 36th. H.T.M.Bty.	1 gun.
108th. Bde. Stokes Mortars	4 guns.

Table of tasks is attached.

2. Zero will be 11.30 a.m.

Watches will be synchronized at 10 a.m. and 11 a.m.

3. Trenches U.8.5. U.8.6. U.8.7. and U.2.1 will be cleared under arrangements by 108th. Inf. Brigade.

4. The Group Commander will be at O.P. B/172 Battery during the operation.

5. A C K N O W L E D G E.

W A Edmenson
Lt.
172nd. Brigade. R.F.A.

14.11.1916.

Copies to

1. B.M.108th. Inf. Bde.
2. B.M.36th.Div.Arty.
3. A/172.
4. B/172.
5. C/172.
6. D/172.
7. Z 36th. T.M.Bty.
8. V 36th. H.T.M.Bty.
9. D.T.M.O.
10. 108th. Stokes Mortars.
11. File.
12. Diary.

T A B L E O F T A S K S.

Battery.	Time.	Task.	Ammn.	Remarks.
A/172.	Minus 2 to Plus 55	Hostile support line from U.2.a.7705 to U.2.a.6028. O.P's at the following points:- U.2.b.0121 U.2.a.6093.	10 A 60 AX	
B/172.	do.	Hostile support line from U.2.a.7705 to U.2.c.8173. O.P's at the following points:- U.2.c.9272. U.2.b.6745. U.2.d.7190.	15 A 75 AX	
D/172.	do.	**Two guns.** Trench Mortar Emplacements:- WALLABY WINTER WILLIE WOODEN WHACKER WHY NOT **Two guns.** Trench Mortar Emplacements:- WHITEBIRD. WENDY WANKER WORSTED WILFRED	150 BX for the whole operation.	
Z 36th. T.M.Bty.	ZERO to plus 15	Hostile front line from U.2.c.6783 to U.2.c.6287.	As many rounds as possible.	Fire to be directed on new enemy work
	Plus 20 to Plus 35	Hostile front line from U.2.c.6287 to U.2.c.6090.		
	Plus 40 to Plus 55	Hostile front line from U.2.c.6090 to U.2.c.6095.		
108th. Stokes Mortar Bty.	ZERO to Plus 15	Hostile front line and communication trenches from U.2.c. 6783 to U.2.c.6095.	5 rounds per gun per minute.	
	Plus 20 to Plus 35	Hostile front line & Communication trenches from U.2.c.6287 to U.2.c.6095.	do.	
	Plus 40 to Plus 55	Hostile front line and communication trenches from U.2.c. 6090 to U.2.a.5010.	do.	
V 36th H.T.M.Bty.	ZERO to Plus 55	Hostile defences from U.8.a.8845 to U.8.a.9789.	As many rounds as possible.	

Instructions regarding War Diaries and Intelligence Summaries are contained in F. S. Regs., Part II. and the Staff Manual respectively. Title pages will be prepared in manuscript.

December 1916

WAR DIARY ~~or INTELLIGENCE SUMMARY.~~ of 172nd Brigade, R.F.A

(Erase heading not required.)

Army Form C. 2118.

Vol / 3

Place	Date	Hour	Summary of Events and Information	Remarks and references to Appendices
In the Field	1/12/16.		Visited trenches and inspected work on 2" T.M. Emplacement and reconnoitred position for 6" T.M. In the afternoon to DRANOUTRE to see 'C' Battery Wagon Line. Weather cold + frosty - very misty.	[illegible]
	2/12/16		Conference at HQ. 153 in the morning. Inspected Horses, harness and Wagon line of "A" very satisfactory display. Weather again misty + cold. App x to [illegible] of Arrangements issued (app1).	[illegible] app I.
	3/12/16		No events, weather cold and misty	[illegible]
	4/12/16		Inspected Battery Positions "A" + "B" and Wagon Line of 'D' consulted with Newcombe as to converting this Wagon Line into 6 gun battery accomodation	[illegible]
	5/12/16		Watched Trench Mortar bombardment, from Fletchers field and then visited both Battalion Headquarters. In the afternoon watched 'B' Battery section training and inspected Wagon Line Weather:- heavy rain in the early morning but sunny + bright after 10 am, much milder	[illegible]

A5834 Wt. W4973/M687 750,000 8/16 D. D. & L. Ltd. Forms/C.2118/13.

2/

Instructions regarding War Diaries and Intelligence Summaries are contained in F. S. Regs., Part II. and the Staff Manual respectively. Title pages will be prepared in manuscript.

WAR DIARY
or
~~INTELLIGENCE SUMMARY.~~
(Erase heading not required.)

Army Form C. 2118.

Place	Date	Hour	Summary of Events and Information	Remarks and references to Appendices
In the Field.	6/11/16		Visited DRANOUTRE in the morning + inspected "C" Battery horses and Wagon Line. Weather, misty + slight rain.	LRLW
	7/11/16.		Inspected temporary T.M. Emplacements in front line and work done on permanent emplacement. Visited both Battalion Commanders and also carried out reconnaissance for T.M. position in Winter Trench. Inspected "D" Battery position in the afternoon. Weather very misty, observation impossible.	LRLW
	8/11/16		Conference at 153 Bde. H.Q. Weather wet during the morning, rather misty but mild.	LRLW
	9/11/16		Carried out reconnaissance for "Winter" scheme. In afternoon inspected, horses, harness + wagon line of D/177. Very Satisfactory. One man of D/177 killed by chance shell. Weather Wet + misty	LRLW
	10/11/16		Visited trenches and inspected work done on permanent Trench Mortar emplacement + dug-out. Also visited Battalion Commanders in line. Observed considerable damage done by hostile retaliation for Trench Mortar bombardment on Friday. Corps Signal Officer went over Group Communications and expressed himself highly pleased. Weather, cloudy, showery + rain.	LRLW

A5834 Wt. W4973/M687 750,000 8/16 D. D. & L. Ltd. Forms/C.2118/13.

3.

Instructions regarding War Diaries and Intelligence Summaries are contained in F. S. Regs., Part II. and the Staff Manual respectively. Title pages will be prepared in manuscript.

WAR DIARY
or
~~INTELLIGENCE SUMMARY.~~

(Erase heading not required.)

Army Form C. 2118.

Place	Date	Hour	Summary of Events and Information	Remarks and references to Appendices
In the Field	11/12/16		Issued Operation orders No. 14 and 15. (Appendices II + III) subsequently cancelled. Inspected wagon line B/172. and found general improvement. Visited Wagon line A/172. and saw Section Training in progress. Weather overcast + raw.	App II, App III, [illegible initials]
	12/12/16		No events of importance. Rain + snow all day.	
	13/12/16		Watched registration of trench mortars on La Petite Douve from O.P B/172. Inspected battery positions "B" + "D" + was present at Section Training "D". In afternoon inspected horses and Wagon line C/172. Weather cloudy and raw. Instructions issued 14a/172 (App IV)	[illegible initials], [illegible initials], App IV
	14/12/16		Spent morning in the trenches visiting Company and Battalion Headquarters + trench mortar position and inspected work done on permanent trench mortar emplacements and dug outs. Weather finer but still cold.	[illegible initials]
	15/12/16		From O.P B/172 watched bombardment of La Petite Douve O.O. 16 issued (Appendix V). Subsequently inspected Wagon line A/172 Battery. In afternoon inspected wagon line "B" Battery and saw their horses. In evening interviewed Trench and Stokes Mortar officers.	[illegible initials], App V, [illegible initials]
	16/12/16		Conference during the morning. In afternoon visited trenches and saw work done on permanent emplacement. Weather cold and frosty.	

A5834 Wt. W4973/M687 750,000 8/16 D. D. & L. Ltd. Forms/C.2118/13.

4

Instructions regarding War Diaries and Intelligence Summaries are contained in F. S. Regs., Part II. and the Staff Manual respectively. Title pages will be prepared in manuscript.

WAR DIARY

~~or~~

~~INTELLIGENCE SUMMARY.~~

(Erase heading not required.)

Army Form C. 2118.

Place	Date	Hour	Summary of Events and Information	Remarks and references to Appendices
In the Field	17/12/16.		Inspected billets of 2/36 T.M. Battery and horses and Wagon line C/172 battery. Weather misty and raw.	LEHW
	18/12/16.		G.O.C in command of 2nd Army inspected all battery positions in the Group. During afternoon visited Section Training "A" and "D" Batteries. Weather misty and cold.	LEHW
	19/12/16.		Carried out reconnaissance for site for 6" Trench Mortar position and dug-outs. Saw both Battalion Commanders. Weather dull and very cold, snow commenced to fall about 3-30 pm.	LEHW
	20/12/16.		Inspection of 109th Infantry Bde. and 36th Divisional Artillery by General Sir Douglas Haig. During the afternoon made inspection of 'A' and 'D' Batteries. As there was good observation – spent some time in observing and reconnoitring hostile defences which show signs of much new work. Weather, bright and clear but very cold, the coldest yet experienced this winter.	LEHW
	21/12/16.		Inspected "A" battery position and "D" Wagon line. Weather dull not so cold, very strong S.W. wind. App x1 to Precis of Arrangements issued (App VI)	LEHW App VI.
	22/12/16.		In the morning inspected wagon lines 'A' and 'B' batteries. In afternoon visited trenches and inspected work done on 6" T.M. Emplacement. Weather windy and showery.	LEHW

5

Instructions regarding War Diaries and Intelligence Summaries are contained in F. S. Regs., Part II. and the Staff Manual respectively. Title pages will be prepared in manuscript.

WAR DIARY
or
~~INTELLIGENCE~~ SUMMARY.
(Erase heading not required.)

Army Form C. 2118.

Place	Date	Hour	Summary of Events and Information	Remarks and references to Appendices
In Field	23/12/16		Conference at 153 Bde Headquarters. Much discussion on various subjects. Very strong gale of wind with heavy showers.	[illegible]
	24/12/16		Rode over to Dranoutre and saw C/172 Wagon Line. Preliminary orders for move received.	[illegible]
	25/12/16		Visited site of new battery position to be occupied by A/172. Decided to occupy with one section only. Enemy heavily shelled 6" Howitzer position near 107th Infantry Bde. H.Q. Fire continued for two hours at about 3 rounds per minute, 5.9" used. No damage done. Weather fine and mild. O.O. 17 issued (App VII)	[illegible] App VII.
	26/12/16		Accompanied C.R.A and C.R.E. in tour of inspection of work carried out on T.M. Emplacements and dug-outs in Group zone. Then proceeded on tour of trenches in new zone. In afternoon proceeded to Irish Farm to watch experimental shoot of 6" T.M. Only 6 rounds fired as hostile retaliation was heavy and accurate. Weather foggy & cold. O.O. No 18 issued (App. VIII)	[illegible] App VIII
	27/12/16		Accompanied by D.T.M.O. and O.C. 2/36 battery, carried out reconnaissance for fresh positions for 6" T.M. and decided on U.8.3. To R.A.H.Q. to discuss designs sent in in connection with standard Gun Pt. A fine day & much milder. O.O. No 19 issued (App IX).	[illegible] App IX.

6.

Instructions regarding War Diaries and Intelligence Summaries are contained in F. S. Regs., Part II. and the Staff Manual respectively. Title pages will be prepared in manuscript.

WAR DIARY
or
~~INTELLIGENCE SUMMARY.~~

(Erase heading not required.)

Army Form C. 2118.

Place	Date	Hour	Summary of Events and Information	Remarks and references to Appendices
In the Field.	28/12/16.		Took over Command of Right Group which is composed of 3-18 pdr batteries and one 4.5 How Battery (6 guns), two medium T.M. and one Heavy T.M. Batteries. At 2-15 pm proceeded to subsidiary to watch experimental shoot of 6" T.M. A successful shoot, 90 rounds being fired. Hostile retaliation was heavy but misdirected. Rear Command opened in Neuve Eglise. Weather foggy and rain. O.O. No 20 issued (App. X).	LEW
	29/12/16.		Visited and inspected C/173 Battery position and new position of A/172. Some trouble with S.O.S lines otherwise communications quite satisfactory. Weather misty - showers - milder.	App X LEW
	30/12/16		Usual conference at H.Q. 157 Bde during the morning. Visited both Battalion H.Q. in the afternoon. Considerable increase in hostile fire to which we replied vigorously. Weather - much rain and high wind.	LEW
	31/12/16		Inspected Battery positions C/173 and C/172 and O.Ps. C/173 and B/172. Saw C/173 fire on S.O.S and Day lines. Work on Communications carried on up to date. Communications have not been satisfactory in new Zone. Visited Brig General, 109 Infy Bde. Weather misty, very dull, wintry, cold. O.O. No 22 issued (App XII).	LEW App XII

L. E. S. Ward.
Lieut Col RFA
Cdg. 172nd Bde R.F.A.

Appendix A to Precis of Arrangements

RIGHT GROUP.

::::::::

The following is the action taken in the event of a GAS ALERT or ENEMY GAS ATTACK:-

Should the gas cloud be unaccompanied by an infantry attack, no S.O.S. signal is sent, but the message "Gas attack", Trench ....

The troops in the front trenches open a slow rate of rifle and machine gun fire at once against the German trenches. All howitzers are turned on to the enemy's trenches from which the gas is being emitted or in which the enemy's infantry may be concentrating for the assault, and a light barrage by 18 pdrs. is put on NO MAN'S LAND to prevent hostile patrols from following up the gas. No intense S.O.S. barrage is employed at this stage.

Should an infantry attack develop, the normal procedure of S.O.S. is carried out.

This cancels para.9. of Precis of Arrangements.

W A Edmenson
Lt. R.F.A.

2.12.1916. Adjt.172nd. Bde. R.F.A.

Copies as for Precis of Arrangements.

Operation Orders No.14. Copy No.________
By
Lieut. Col. L.E.S.Ward, D.S.O., R.F.A.
Commanding Centre Group.
:::::::::

SECRET.

36th. Divisional Artillery Order No.35.

1. A Bombardment of enemy trenches will take place at 10 a.m. on Tuesday, 12th. instant.

Right and Centre Groups will arrange to synchronize watches at 8 a.m.

2. TheBatteries to be employed are A, B & D Batteries, 113th. Brigade, R.F.A., and A, B & D Batteries, 172nd. Brigade. R.F.A.

3. The 18 pdr. Batteries will use H.E. and endeavour to destroy the enemy's parapet.

4. The 4.5" Howitzers will bombard hostile Trench Mortar emplacements as detailed

5. Ammunition available -

200 rounds A.X. per 18 pdr. Battery.
100 do.BX per 4.5" Howitzer Battery.

6. Distribution of fire -
A & B Batteries, 113th. Brigade R.F.A.
On Support Line U.8.b.4045 - U.8.b.3060

A & B Batteries 172nd. Brigade. R.F.A.

On Support Line U.8.b.3060 - U.8.b.2377

D/113th. Brigade R.F.A., on Trench Mortars WILFRED & WANKER
D/172 do. do. WENDY & WHY NOT

7. As this bombardment is intended for the destruction of the enemy's parapet and Trench Mortar emplacements, fire should be opened at a slow rate and each gun individually corrected; the rate of fire being quickened later.
The bombardment will be completed by 10.45 a.m.

8. A C K N O W L E D G E.

11.12.1916. sd. B.M.36th. Div. Arty.

(2)

To:- A,B & D Batts.(108th. Inf. Bde. for information)

In accordance with the above operation order

"B" Battery will fire on Support Line from U.8.b.3060 to U.8.b.3069.
"A" do. do. U.8.b.3069 to U.8.b.2377.
"D" do. do. WENDY and WHY NOT.

Signal time will be sent out at 8 and 9 a.m.

W.A.Edmenson.

Lt. R.F.A.
Adjt.172nd. Bde. R.F.A

11.12.1916.

Operation Orders No. 22

by

Lieut. Col. L.L.S. Ward, D.S.O., R.F.A.,

Commanding 172nd Brigade R.F.A. 31-12-16.

Ref. Mp. PLOEGSTEERT 1/10,000.

1. The 6" Trench Mortar will fire a series of 100 rounds on the hostile trenches from U.8.b.2020 to U.8.b.0020 (Salient angle included), on the 1st Jany.17.

2. The Operation will commence as soon after 1-30 p.m. as possible.

3. B/172 Battery, (6 guns) C/173 Battery (6 guns) and D/172 Battery (4 guns) will stand by to punish hostile retaliation.

B/172 Battery will fire on the hostile support line from U.8.b.4821 to U.8.b.2063.

C/173 Battery will fire on the hostile front line from U.8.b.4513to U.8.d.9863.

Fire will be opened in immediate return for hostile retaliation and will be given in bursts of from three to four rounds gun-fire. Allotment of ammunition, up to 60 rounds per battery if necessary.

D/172 will engage any hostile trench mortars which become active during the operation. Allotment of ammunition, 40 rounds.

4. A C K N O W L E D G E.

W.A. Edmenson

Lieut. R.F.A.,
Adjt. 172nd Bde. R.F.A.

Copies to :-

1. B.M. 36th Div. Arty.
2. B.M. 109th Inf. Bde.
3. D.T.M.O.
4. O.C. Z/36 T.M. BTy.
5. O.C. B/172.
6. O.C. D/172.
7. O.C. C/173.
8. File.
9. Diary.

Operation Orders No.15. Copy No______

By

Lieut. Col. L.E.S.Ward, D.S.O., R.F.A.

Commanding Centre Group.

::::::::::::::::::

Ref. Map. PLOEGSTEERT 1/10,000 11th. December, 1916.

1. A bombardment of the hostile defences will take place on Thursday, December 14th.1916.

The following Units will take part:-

B/172 - 18pdr. Battery		
D/172. - 4.5" Howitzer Battery		
One 4.5" Howitzer Battery of Right Group		
X/36th. T.M.Battery	3	guns
Y/36th. T.M.Battery	3	guns
Z/36th. T.M.Battery	3	guns
V/36th. H.T.M.Battery	2	guns
107th. Stokes Mortar Battery	4	guns
108th. Stokes Mortar Battery	4	guns
109th. Stokes Mortar Battery	4	guns

2. ZERO will be at 5 a.m.

Watches will be synchronized at 10 p.m. on night 13th/14th. December, and at 4 a.m. 14th. December.

3. Table of Tasks is attached.

4. Officers Commanding Units taking part will render a written report on the operation to Centre Group Headquarters before 2 p.m. 14th.December.

5. Trenches U.8.4., U.8.5., U.8.6., U.8.7,. and Winter Trench from U.8.a.2013 to U.8.a.0010. will be cleared under arrangements by 108th and 109th. Infantry Brigades

6. The trenches mentioned in para.5. will be cleared when registration is being carried out by T.M's.

7. O.C. Centre Group will be at O.P. D/172 Battery during the operation.

8. ACKNOWLEDGE

Lt. R.FA
Adjt.172nd. Bde. R.F.A

11.12.1916.

Copies to

1. B.M.36th. Div. Arty.
2. B.M.107th. Inf.Bde.
3. B.M.108th. Inf. Bde.
4. B.M.109th.Inf. Bde.
5. B/172
6. D/172.
7. O.C.Right Group.
8. X/36th. T.M.Bty
9. Y/36th. T.M.Bty.
10. Z/36th. T.M.Bty.
11. V/36th. H.T.M.Bty.
12. D.T.M.O.
13. File.
14. Diary.

OPERATION ORDER NO. 17.,

By.

LIEUT.,COL. L.E.S. WARD. D.S.O.,R.F.A.,

Cdg. CENTRE GROUP.

Ref. Map. PLOEGSTEERT. 1/10000 25-12-16.

1. An experimental bombardment with one 6" Trench Mortar will take place on Tuesday December 26th at 2-30 p.m. and Wednesday December 27th at 10-30 a.m.

The duration of the bombardment will be 30 minutes.

2. The points to be bombarded will be from U.8.b.0016 to U.8.a.9427 (salient angle included) on Tuesday and strong point about U.8.a.9070 on Wednesday.

3. B/172 Battery will cover the 6" Trench Mortar during both operations firing on the hostile defences from U.8.b.2284 to U.2.d.5062. Allotment of ammunition 50 rounds AX for each day.

D/172 will engage hostile trench mortars, WHIPPET, WILFRED, and any others thatbecome active during the operations. Allotment of ammunition 20 rounds BX each day.

Covering fire will commence 2 minutes before the T.M. opens fire.

A/172 Battery will stand by for bombardment of enemy defences from U.2.a.5040 to U.2.c.9088, in the event of his retaliating strongly for the 6" T.M.

4 In each series the first 10 rounds will be fired for registration and experimental observation, after which the fire will be for effect.

5. Watches will be synchronized at 2 p.m. Dec. 26th and 10 a.m. Dec. 27th.

6. Trenches U.8.5. and U.8.6. are being cleared under arrangements by Brigade Major, 108th Infy. Brigade.

7. The Heavy Group is being asked to stand by for Counter Battery Work if required.

8. A C K N O W L E D G E.

W.A. Edmenson.
Lieut. R.F.A.,
Adjt. 172nd Bde. R.F.A.

28-12-16.

Copies to :-

1. B.M. 36th Div. Arty.
2. B.M. 108th Infy. Bde.
3. B.M. 109th Infy. Bde.
4. D.T.M.O.
5. O.C. Z/36 T.M. Bty.
6. O.C. A/172.
7. O.C. B/172.
8. O.C. D/172.
9. File.
10. Diary.

S E C R E T.

Operation Orders No,16. Copy________

by

Lieut. Col. L.E.S. Ward, D.S.O., R.F.A.,

Commanding Centre Group. 16-12-16.

1. B. and D. Batteries, 113 Bde. R.F.A. will be relieved by A. and C. Batteries, 172nd Brigade R.F.A., respectively on the 27th and 28th instant.

2. Reliefs will be carried out in accordance with the attached Appendix "A" and will be completed on the night of 28/29th December 1916.

3. Guns will not be handed over.

4. Registrations, Trench Maps etc in connection with the fronts covered will be handed and taken over.

5. Ammunition will be handed and taken over as follows :-

B/113 Battery to A/172 Battery.

D/113 Battery to C/172 Battery.

O.C. A/172 Battery will return to O.C. D.A.C. the same amount of ammunition taken over from B/113 Battery.

Ammunition for Section taking over new position will be supplied, either out of the existing stock at present position or a quantity of that ~~handed~~ handed over by B/113 Battery will be taken on A/172 Battery stock and a similar amount returned to O.C. D.A.C.

O.C. C/172 Battery will hand over all ammunition at present in his carriages to O.C. D/173 Battery.

Ammunition will pass and will be reported to this Office not later than 9a.m. 28th instant.

Copies of receipts given and taken to be handed into this Office not later than 9 a.m. 29th instant.

6. Telephone Offices will be taken and handed over with exchange boards and receipts given and obtained. Copies of receipts to be in this Office by 9 a.m. 29th instant.

7. H.Q. 172nd Brigade R.F.A. will move to T.14.d.8090 at 6-30 p.m. on the 28th instant.

8. No move will take place on either day before 4-30 p.m.

Appendix "A" to Centre Group Operation Orders No.18.

Table of Reliefs evening 27/28th Dec.

Unit.	Relieves.	Remarks.
One Section A/172 Batty.	One Section B/113 Batty.	
One Section C/172 Batty.	One Section D/113 Batty.	This Section comes under control of D/103 after relief is completed.

Table of Reliefs evening 28/29th Dec.

Unit.	Relieves.	Remarks.
Two Sections A/172 Batty. (Which remain in present position)	Two Sections B/113 Batty.	
One Section C/172 Batty.	One Section D/113 Batty.	This Section comes under control of D/172 after relief is completed.

H.Q. 172. To T.14.d.30PG.

Operation Orders No. 19. Copy No.____

by

Lieut. Col. L.E.S. Ward, D.S.O., R.F.A.,

Commanding CENTRE GROUP. 27-12-17.

Ref. Map. PLOEGSTEERT 1/10,000.

1. An experimental bombardment with one 6" Trench Mortar, firing from trench U.8.3. bay 9., will take place on Thursday December 28th at 2-15 p.m.

The duration of the bombardment will be 45 minutes.

2. The point to be bombarded will be from U.8.b.0016 to U.8.a.9427 (salient angle included).

3. B/172 Battery will cover the 6" Trench Mortar during the operation, firing on the hostile defences from U.8.b.2284 to U.2.d.5062. Allotment of ammunition 50 rounds AX.

D/172 Battery will fire with two guns on PETITE DOUVE area from U.8.a.8655 to U.8.a.9065, and WINTER and WILFRED with remaining section. Should any others become active during the operation, the section firing on PETITE DOUVE will switch on to them. Allotment of ammunition 40 rounds BX.

Covering fire will commence two minutes before the Trench Mortar opens fire.

X. A Battery of 113 Brigade R.F.A. will stand by for bombardment of enemy trenches in the event of his retaliating strongly for the Trench Mortar.

4. The Trench Mortar will fire the first ten rounds for registration and experimental observation, after which fire will be for effect.

5. Watches will be synchronized at 1-30 p.m. Dec. 28th.

6. WESBORNE AVENUE, WINTER TRENCH and trench W.8.3. are being cleardd under arrangements by Brigade Major, 109th Infy. Brigade.

7. The Heavy Group is being asked to stand by for Counter Battery Work if required.

8. A C K N O W L E D G E.

W.A. Edmenson.
Lieut. R.F.A.,
Adjt. 172nd Bde. R.F.A.

Copies to :-

1. B.M. 36 Div. Arty.
2. B.M. 108 Inf. Bde.
3. B.M. 109 Inf. Bde.
4. O.C. 113 Bde.R.F.A.
5. D.T.M.O.
6. O.C. Z/36 T.M.Bty.
7. O.C. A/172.
8. O.C. B/172.
9. O.C. D/172.
10. File.
11. Diary.

Right Group Orders No. 20

by

Lieut. Col. L.E.S. Ward, D.S.O., R.F.A.,

Commanding RIGHT GROUP. 28-12-16.

Ref. Map. PLOEGSTEERT 1/10,000.

1. Composition. The Group is composed as follows:-

A/172	18-pdr Battery.	6 guns.
B/172	do.	6 do.
C/173	do.	6 do.
D/172	4.5." How. Battery.	4 do.
x 1 Section C/172	do.	2 do.

x Note. This Section is under the tactical command of O.C. D/172.

Z/36	2" Trench Mortar Battery.	4 guns.
X/36	do.	4 do.
V/36	Heavy Trench Mortar Battery	2 do.

2. Distribution. The Group covers the sector held by the 109th Infy Brigade, extending from ANTONS FARM to junction of trenches U.1.2. and U.1.3.

The Group zone on the hostile front extends from LE ROSSIGNOL - ANTONS FARM- BLACKSHEDS ROAD, inclusive to the STINKING FARM - MESSINES ROAD inclusive.

The dividing line between right and left sub-sectors is the point where the river DOUVE crosses our front line.

C/173 Battery will cover the Right Company Right Sub-Sector. Zone on hostile front line - from U.15.a.4078 (LE ROSSIGNOL - ANTONS FARM - BLACKSHEDS ROAD inclusive) to U.8.d.7985, trench junction inclusive.

Battalion Headquarters are at LIMAVADY LODGE.

Company Headquarters are at U.8.d.2520.

B/172 Battery will cover the Left Company Right Sub-Sector and Right Company Left Sub-Sector,

Zone on hostile front line - from U.8.d.7985 (trench junction inclusive) to U.8.a.5780.

2.
Distribution Cond.

Battalion Headquarters are at LIMAVADY LODGE and LA PLUS DOUVE FARM.

Company Headquarters are at U.8.a.2005.

A/172 Battery will cover the Left Company Left Sub-Sector.

Zone on hostile front line - from U.8.a.9780 to the MESSINES - STINKING FARM ROAD inclusive.

Battalion Headquarters are at LA PLUS DOUVE FARM.

Company Headquarters are at U.1.d.7560.

Battery Commanders will select points for S.O.S., creeping barrage (Night Lines) and Red Hand (Day Lines) and forward them to Group Headquarters as soon as possible.

D/172 Battery will cover the whole Group zone.

The following will be the S.O.S. (Night Lines) points for this Battery.

U.15.a.3089.	Junction of sap with front line.
U.8.d.7586.	Junction of communication trench with front line.
U.8.b.4042.	Junction of Trenches.
U.8.a.9274	Strong point in hostile front line.
U.2.d.1252	Junction of trenches.
U.2.c.9295	Junction of trenches.

The O.C. D/172 Battery will select points for Red Hand (Day Lines) and forward them to Group Headquarters as soon as possible.

All Batteries will lay on S.O.S. (Night Lines) at 6-30 p.m. December 28th 1916.

3.
Mutual Support.

(a) Support of Left Group 36th Division :-

A/172 Battery will barrage hostile front line from U.2.c.5893 to U.2.a.1070.

D/172 Battery will put one howitzer on the Barrier U.2.a.1090 and one howitzer on NESTOR TRENCH U.2.a.5065.

(b) Support from Left Group 36th Division.

One 18-pdr Battery will barrage from the STINKING

3.
Mutual Support (Contd).

FARM- MESSINES ROAD to U.2.d.1210.

One howitzer will fire on trench junction at U.2.d.1252 and one howitzer on trench junction at.U.2.c.9295.

(c) Support of Left Group fo Division on our Right to be arranged.

~~xxxxxxxx~~ (d) Support from Left Group of Division on our Right.

One 18-pdr Battery will barrage hostile front line from ANTONS FARM - BLACKSHEDS ROAD to U.8.d.7985.

One howitzer will fire on junction of sap with front line at U.15.a.3089 and one howitzer on junction of communication trench with front line at U.8.d.7586.

Calls for Mutual Support in above cases will be :-

A. "Support Left Group".

B. " do. Right Group".

C. " d. Left Group, 25th Division."

D. " do. Right Group, 36 Division ".

4.
Communications. The Officer in charge Group Signals will arrange for the following :-

(a) Right Bttalion H.Q.
Right Company, Right Sub-Sector.
With C/173.

(b) Right Battalion H.Q.
Left Battalion H.Q.
Left Company, Right Sub-Sector.
Right Company, Left Sub-Sector
With B/172.

(c) Left Batalion H.Q.
Left Company, Left Sub-Sector.
With A/172.

5.
S.O.S. Lines. S.O.S. Lines for all Trench Mortars Batteries in the Group will remain the same until furthers orders are issued.

6.
O.Ps. Batteries will make no change in their O.Ps for the present.

7. Group H.Q. Command at Group H.Q. will open at 6-30 p.m. 28th instant at T.14.d.8090.

8. 108 Inf. Bde. New artillery distribution will come into force on Dec. 28th, but during the night Dec. 28/29th 108th Infantry Brigade will still be in position and will be in communocation with Right and Left Group H.Q.

9. Liaison. C/172 Battery will find Liaison Officer at LIMAVADY LODGE tonight, reporting there before 7 p.m.

10. A C K N O W L E D G E.

Issued at 1-30 p.m.
28th Dec. 1916.

W.A. Edmenson
Lieut. R.F.A.,
Adjt. 172nd Bde. R.F.A.

Copies to :-

1. B.M. 36th Div. Arty.
2. B.M. 109th Inf. Bde.
3. B.M. 108th Inf. Bde.
4. D.T.M.O.
5. C/173.
6. A/172.
7. B/172.
8. C/172.
9. D/172.
10. 153 Bde. R.F.A.
11. File.
12 Diary.

Instructions regarding War Diaries and Intelligence Summaries are contained in F. S. Regs., Part II. and the Staff Manual respectively. Title pages will be prepared in manuscript.

WAR DIARY
or
INTELLIGENCE SUMMARY.
(Erase heading not required.)

Army Form C. 2118.

172 Bde RFA

Vol 14

Place	Date	Hour	Summary of Events and Information	Remarks and references to Appendices
In the Field	1/1/17		made tour of O.Ps A" - B and D/172 Bde and saw each Battery fire on S.O.S and day lines. In the afternoon, accompanied by Lieut Pinto carried out reconnaissance for battery positions for Counter attack on hill 63. Much activity on both sides in Artillery. D/172 Howitzer battery bombarded enemy's lines with effect. Weather - overcast, no rain, mild. Att'd S.O.S. [illegible] round (app I)	App I [illegible]
	2/1/17		Inspected B/172 battery position and went on to B/172 O.P. to observe 6" T.M. Shoot. The enemy very quickly located the position of the gun and made it impossible for the practice to be continued. 37 rounds were fired, many "blinds" occurred. Accompanied by A.D.V.S. inspected all horses of A" - B" and D" batteries which were "led by" unrugged. Very satisfactory inspection. Weather - fine - good observation - Temp. very mild.	
	3/1/17		Met O.C. A/172 and 1?? Field Coy R.E. on proposed new site of battery position. Accompanied C.R.A. on inspection of B/172 Wagon Lines. Most satisfactory inspection. In the afternoon went to Dranoutre and saw horses of C/172 "led by" unrugged -	

A5834 Wt. W4973/M687 750,000 8/16 D. D. & L. Ltd. Forms/C.2118/13.

Instructions regarding War Diaries and Intelligence Summaries are contained in F. S. Regs., Part II. and the Staff Manual respectively. Title pages will be prepared in manuscript.

WAR DIARY
or
INTELLIGENCE SUMMARY.
(Erase heading not required.)

Army Form C. 2118.

Place	Date	Hour	Summary of Events and Information	Remarks and references to Appendices
In the Field	3/1/17		Considering circumstances, very fair. Considerable decrease in our own and hostile fire during the day. Weather – overcast and cloudy – windy.	
	4/1/17		Made tour of trenches visiting Battalion HQ at La Plus Douve Farm, Company Headquarters left subsection and also inspected work done on Trench Mortar Emplacements and dug-outs. Then proceeded along Winter trench to 6" TM emplacement and part of right subsector. Hostile artillery much quieter on our front trenches but displayed some activity on back blocks. A/172 battery shelled with a few 15 cm. Weather – steady rain in the morning but general clear up about midday – afternoon bright.	
	5/1/17		Intimation received that the Brigade would be broken up to reinforce Army Troops. Visited A and D/172 and C/173 battery positions and wagon line D/172 – also made inspection of Bde. HQ horses and wagon line generally. Following officers "mentioned" in despatches Jan 3rd Lieut Col Ward, Lieuts. Champion	

A5834 Wt. W4973/M687 750,000 8/16 D. D. & L. Ltd. Forms/C.2118/13.

Instructions regarding War Diaries and Intelligence Summaries are contained in F. S. Regs., Part II. and the Staff Manual respectively. Title pages will be prepared in manuscript.

WAR DIARY
or
INTELLIGENCE SUMMARY.
(Erase heading not required.)

Army Form C. 2118.

Place	Date	Hour	Summary of Events and Information	Remarks and references to Appendices
In the Field	5/1/17		and Edmonson. Weather fine & sunny – colder. Appendices to order No 20 issued (App II)	
	6/1/17		Conference at 153 Bde HQ. Both artilleries very quiet. Infantry much pleased and work on trenches progressing favourably. Weather – fine & sunny.	App II.
	7/1/17		Very quiet day on the whole. Concentrations A & B fired at request of Infantry. Champion proceeded on leave. Weather – cold and bright – no rain.	
	8/1/17		Made tour of trenches visiting company and battalion headquarters and trench mortars at Seaforth and Anton's Farms. A quiet day for both artilleries. Attended lecture at Bailleul. Weather – Clear and bright in the morning changing to rain and sleet in the afternoon.	
	9/1/17		Visited wagon lines "A" and "B" batteries and battery position of "A". Weather clear and mild.	
	10/1/17		Inspected battery position "B" and C/173, and wagon line D/172. Weather fine in the morning, changing to sleet in the afternoon.	

A5834 Wt. W4973/M687 750,000 8/16 D. D. & L. Ltd. Forms/C.2118/13.

Army Form C. 2118.

WAR DIARY
or
INTELLIGENCE SUMMARY.
(Erase heading not required.)

Instructions regarding War Diaries and Intelligence Summaries are contained in F. S. Regs., Part II. and the Staff Manual respectively. Title pages will be prepared in manuscript.

Place	Date	Hour	Summary of Events and Information	Remarks and references to Appendices
Inkle Field	11/1/17		Inspected 'D' battery position. Both artillery very quiet – Weather overcast but no rain until evening	
	12/1/17		General Brock made tour of batteries to say goodbye. Weather – alternating rain and fine. Signal Officer 173 arrived to take over Communications	
	13/1/17		Visited 'B' Battery O.P and Positions in morning. Visited 'C' battery wagon line afternoon. Weather fine with a little rain.	
	14/1/17		Weather – very wet and cloudy. Situation very quiet	
	15/1/17		Advance party of 173rd Brigade R.F.A arrived. Received orders to take over Temporary Command of 180 Bde RFA. Weather fine with slight frost	
	16/1/17		Visited batteries to say goodbye before proceeding to 180 Bde RFA. Moved from Neuve Eglise to T.11.d.21 and took over old billets. Tactical Command ceased at 6-30pm. Weather fine but hazy slight frost. 'B' battery left position and proceeded to Wagon Line.	
	17/1/17		Proceeded to 180 Bde RFA to take over Command Major Bolitho	

A5834 Wt. W4973/M687 750,000 8/16 D. D. & L. Ltd. Forms/C.2118/13.

Army Form C. 2118.

Instructions regarding War Diaries and Intelligence Summaries are contained in F. S. Regs., Part II. and the Staff Manual respectively. Title pages will be prepared in manuscript.

WAR DIARY
or
~~INTELLIGENCE SUMMARY.~~

(Erase heading not required.)

Place	Date	Hour	Summary of Events and Information	Remarks and references to Appendices
In the Field	17/1/17		taking over Command of 17nd Bde RFA "A" Battery tactically under command of 173rd Bde RFA Weather fine with rain alternations	
	18/1/17		Weather heavy fall of snow during night and continued during the day.	
	19/1/17		Weather, snow still lying, hardened by frost, clear & bright	
	20/1/17		Weather, bright & sunny, frost holding.	
	21/1/17		Received orders for re-organisation to be carried out on basis on 23rd January 1917 Later received wire to take no action eventually Cancelled Weather still frosty, bright & clear	
	22/1/17		Re-organisation orders returned to Div Arty Weather as 21-1-17	
	23/1/17		Conference held at Bde Headquarters re mange amongst horses Weather no change	
	24/1/17		Lieut Edmonson proceeded on leave Weather still frosty and very cold Fine with sunshine	

A5834 Wt. W4973/M687 750,000 8/16 D. D. & L. Ltd. Forms/C.2118/13.

Instructions regarding War Diaries and Intelligence Summaries are contained in F. S. Regs., Part II. and the Staff Manual respectively. Title pages will be prepared in manuscript.

WAR DIARY
or
~~INTELLIGENCE SUMMARY.~~
(Erase heading not required.)

Army Form C. 2118.

Place	Date	Hour	Summary of Events and Information	Remarks and references to Appendices
In the Field	25/1/17		Nothing to report. Weather unchanged.	
	26/1/17		B/177 sends one section into action on left of B/153 and another to replace gun of A/177 put out of action by hostile fire. Weather cold but fine. Wind dangerous.	
	27/1/17		HQ. Office and officers mess moved up to Neuve Eglise - Wagon lines to remain at St James Farm owing to existence of mange. M.O. Lt Glanville RAMC returns from Sanitary Course. Weather cold but fine - Wind dangerous	
	28/1/17		O.C. Bde visits neighbourhood of YPRES to reconnoitre positions for 113 Bde. Heavy bombardment from 6-7-30pm in direction of ARMENTIERES. Weather unchanged.	
	29/1/17		O.C. Bde visits BAILLEUL and holds Conference of Battery Commanders of 113 Bde in the evening. HQ horses washed for mange, under Vet. arrangements. Orders received for disbanding of D/177 - Weather unchanged.	
	30/1/17		Finals of 16 Div Boxing Contest in BAILLEUL - Weather slight fall of snow in afternoon. Still frosty	

A5834 Wt. W4973/M687 750,000 8/16 D. D. & L. Ltd. Forms/C.2118/13.

Instructions regarding War Diaries and Intelligence Summaries are contained in F. S. Regs., Part II. and the Staff Manual respectively. Title pages will be prepared in manuscript.

WAR DIARY
or
~~INTELLIGENCE~~ SUMMARY.

(Erase heading not required.)

Army Form C. 2118.

Place	Date	Hour	Summary of Events and Information	Remarks and references to Appendices
In the Field	31/1/17		D/172 Battery disbanded at 12 noon today slight fall of snow in the night, weather otherwise unchanged.	
			31/1/17 [illegible] Major RFA Cdg 172nd Bde RFA	

A5834 Wt. W4973/M687 750,000 8/16 D. D. & L. Ltd. Forms/C.2118/13.

SECRET.

Appendix 1 to Operation Order No. 22.

RIGHT GROUP.

;;;;;;;;;;;

This operation will take place tomorrow the 2nd January 1917.

Zero time will be 12 noon.

A C K N O W L E D G E.

W.A. Edmenson.
Lieut. R.F.A.,
Adjt. 172nd Bde. R.F.A.

1-1-17.

Copies to :-

1. B.M. 36 Div. Arty.
2. B.M. 109 Inf. Bde.
3. D.T.M.O.
4. O.C. Z/36 T.M. Batty.
5. O.C. B/172.
6. O.C. D/172.
7. O.C. C/173.
8. File.
9. Diary.

6.

Appendix to Right Group Operation Order No. 20.

1. In future A/172 Battery will cover the two Companies holding the Left Sub-Sector and occupying trenches U.5.5. U.6.6., U.6.7., U.2.1. and U.1.2. Zone on hostile front line from U.[illegible].a.9720 to U.[illegible].9780. Company Headquarters at U.[illegible] (F.4.4) and trenches U.2.3., U.1.1. and U.1.2. Zone on hostile front line from U.[illegible].a.9780 to the [illegible] FARM - MESSINES ROAD inclusive. Company Headquarters at U.1.d.7560. (F.Q.6).

2. B/172 Battery will cover the Left Company, Right Sub-Sector, occupying trenches U.8.2. Bay 8, [illegible].3., U.8.4. and WINTER TRENCH. Zone on hostile front line from U.8.d.7985 (trench junction inclusive) to U.[illegible].9720. Company Headquarters at U.8.a.2005.(G.F.5).

3. The Officer in charge of Group Communications will arrange for the necessary changes involved in this re-distribution.

W.A. Jameson

Lieut. R.F.A.,
Adjt. 172nd Bde. R.F.A.

5-1-17.

Copies to:-

1. H.Q. 36 Div. Arty.
2. H.Q. 109 Inf. Bde.
3. A/172.
4. B/172.
5. File.
6. Diary.

www.ingramcontent.com/pod-product-compliance
Lightning Source LLC
Chambersburg PA
CBHW081528160426
43191CB00011B/1713